BIRMINGHAM HISTORICAL SOCIETY

Downtown DISCOVERY TOUR

with *History Hunts*

Third Edition in honour of Patricia Hough Camp & Marjorie Lee White

With the financial support of the
Susan Mott Webb Charitable Trust, Alabama Power Foundation
Community Foundation of Greater Birmingham
City of Birmingham, Alabama Historical Commission

Birmingham Realty Company in honor of its 125th Anniversary

Acknowledgements

The third edition of the Downtown Discovery Tour is dedicated to Pat Camp and to Marjorie Lee White whose commitment to community service got and keeps this tour, and the Society, going.

The creation and publishing of this book has been assisted by a very large number of individuals. Principal helpers include current and former Downtown Discovery Tours guides, volunteers who decided we should expand and reprint the volume, filling it with everything they wanted to tell students on their tours! Russell Cunningham at Birmingham Realty Company gave the lead gift in honor of that company's 125th anniversary. The volume has been a long time coming.

Marjorie Lee White recruited and inspired the reprint and the extraordinary volunteer participation that fills its pages. She and Regan Huff later helped conceptualize the new heritage hikes. Providing research, drawing, and photography were volunteers Kyle D'Agostino, Kyle Kirkwood, Edgar Marx, Jr., Kelly McLaughlin, Beverly Miller, Cheryl Morgan, Michelle Morgan, Kris Nikolich, Carole Sanders, and Peggy Scott. Katherine Parker Shepherd illustrated the time line; Michelle Morgan and Kelly McLaughlin the glossary. Rick Sprague photographed for the original book; Bill and Sloan Dixon, Kyle Kirkwood, John O'Hagan, Bode Morin and Marjorie White for this edition.

Elizabeth Webb Collier, Alicia McGiveran, and especially Peggy Balch did yeoman duty researching and fact-checking data. Proof readers included: Regina Almon, Peggy Balch, Rhonda Covington, Sloan Dixon, Nick Patterson, Kay Henkell Smith and Joe Strickland.

The 25th Anniversary of the tours coincides with the 25th anniversary of the establishment of the Birmingham Public Library Department of Archives & Manuscripts.

Hats off to the City of Birmingham and library administrators and staff who created and expanded this fine institution. Yolanda Valentin, Don Veasey, and Jim Baggett deserve A+++ for endless searches for the best images for this volume. Yvonne Crumpler and the staff at Southern History also cheerfully helped us. All historic photographs in this volume are Archives' photographs unless otherwise identified.

For assistance with documentation and permissions for this publication, we thank Lola Hendricks; Victor Blackledge; Kirkwood Balton, Rose Walker, Booker T. Washington Insurance Co.; Arnold Steiner; Carlton Reese, Director, The Alabama Movement for Human Rights Freedom Choir; Mrs. Ralph Abernathy, Atlanta; David Stokes, Southern Christian Leadership Conference, Atlanta; Jennifer Kruse, Intellectual Properties Management, Inc., Atlanta, Georgia, as manager of the King Estate; Stephanie Hardy, *The Birmingham News*; Nadia Rozina, Black Star; Alyssa Sachar, Corbis/Bettman; Fotofolio, New York; DOWNTOWN Words and Music by Tony Hatch, Copyright 1964 Welbeck Music Ltd. administered by Universal-MCA Music Publishing, a division of Universal Studios, Inc. (ASCAP) International Copyright Secured, All Rights Reserved, Paul Brooks, Assoc. Manager of Music Clearance.

Last and best, artist and graphic designer Scott Fuller made the project possible.

Marjorie L. White

Birmingham Historical Society
White, Marjorie L.
ISBN (softback) O-943994-25-X
Library of Congress 2001 130945

Table of Contents

About the Discovery Tour Book

This book is a guide for DISCOVERING the architecture and history of Birmingham's city center. It contains background information, maps, a time line, a glossary and visuals to encourage looking at and thinking about buildings and urban change.

The guide is intended for school groups, families and the general public.

The self-guided explorations begin at city center cultural institutions and the Birmingham Realty Company, the real estate firm that founded our city in 1871.

These tours, information and lesson plans for teachers also appear on the Birmingham Historical Society web-site at www.bhistorical.org.

Tours

The Downtown Discovery Tour, the central business district

Linn Park History Hunt, the 20th Street park & governmental center

Going Downtown History Hunt, the historic retail & theater district

Fourth Avenue History Hunt, the historic black business district

A Walk to Freedom, retracing the children's marches of 1963

Starting Points

Birmingham Realty Company

Birmingham Museum of Art
Birmingham Public Library

McWane Center
The Alabama Theater

Jazz Hall of Fame
Fourth Avenue Visitor Center

Birmingham Civil Rights Institute
16th Street Baptist Church

GOALS

Discovery

Participation

Visual awakening

Creating architectural understanding

Creating historical understanding
Personalities
Making & remaking buildings & cities

Creating appreciation
Fine quality buildings
Taking care of them

LESSONS

Learning to look at buildings . . .
To visually explore buildings by focusing on architectural details & construction materials: brick, terra cotta & cast iron.

Experiencing architecture . . .
Touching, feeling, going inside & enjoying buildings.

Learning to read buildings & the stories they have to tell . . .
Stories of the people who built them, the stylistic choices they made for their decoration & use, and of how a building's looks change.

THE DOWNTOWN DISCOVERY TOURS
Where They Start & Go

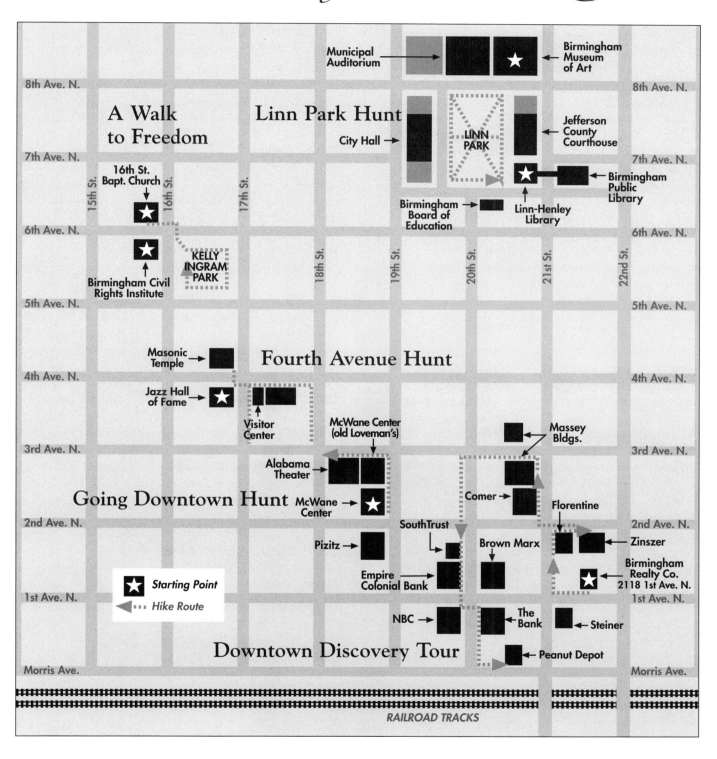

Volunteers Make the Tours Possible

This edition of the tour provides information to encourage school and familiy groups to make self-guided explorations. Over the past 25 years volunteers have made materials and guided tours possible.

For a decade, the Junior League of Birmingham provided start-up funding and volunteers. **Junior League volunteer guides** (*=chairman): Cathy Adams, Mims Adams, Laurie Alverson, Nancy Bagby, *Juju Beale, Pam Beckman, Judy Bewley, Elna Brendel, Betsy Brown, Ann Camp, 1st*Pat Camp, Lucy Carey, Marie Carlisle, Joan Clark, Nancy Cox, Mary Todd Davis, Pat Day, Anna Donald, Isabelle Dreher, *Patsy Dreher, Betts Drennen, Geny Duffee, Terry Estes, Wendy Field, Nancy Gillespy, Judy Gohlson, Tandy Graves, *Kit Hamilton, Terry Hamilton, Pat Harris, *Betsy Blair Hunter, Annette Johnston, Dru Jones,*Lavonda Keel, Brenda Knapp, Gordon Lanier, Connie Lankford, Anna Lee,*Anne Liles, *Mary Evelyn McKee, Louise McPhillips, Koko Mackin, Brucie Mancuso, Nancy Mason, Katherine Shannon Owens, 2nd*Diana Plosser, Anne Proctor, Milner Noel, Ellen Patterson, Ann Proctor, Betsy Rackley, Carolyn Ray, Susie Stockham, Laura Susan Roberts, *Catherine Schiesz, Missy Scott, Katherine Parker Shepherd, Ellen Slaughter, Betsy Smith, *Betty Boyd Sullivan, Libby Tarpley, Lee Van Tassel, Carlyn Turner, *Susan Warnock, Rose Ann Waters, Marjorie White, Jenny Whitmire, Kim Wilcox, Ellen Williams, *Susan Williams, Kim Yarborough, Valentine Yarborough and Peggy Shook Zeiger.

For years, **Birmingham Chapter of the American Institute of Architects volunteers** led tours, illustrated the tour take-home map (Marzette Fischer) and conducted follow-up activities in area classrooms, helping organize and staff the Buddy Up for Building Architectural Awareness program. Architect volunteers: Kyle D'Agostina, Jeff Barton, Paul Bates, Nolanda Bearden, Bob Burns, Paul Callan, Jamie Collins, Donald Cosby, Don Cosper, Marzette Fischer, Jason Fondren, Roman Gary, Eddie Griffith, Wayne Hester, Marina Hobbs, Jeff Johnston, David Jones, Jack Jolley, Kyle Kirkwood, Bruce Lanier, Kelly McLaughlin, Louise McPhillips, Willie Oliver, Ken Ownes, Kris Nikolich, Lawrence Partridge, Charles Penuel, Dean Robinson, Katherine Shannon, Doug Shaddix, Jerry Shadix, Allen Tichansky, and Wayne Williams. Auburn University Center for Architecture and Urban Studies faculty and students also supported Buddy Up Program.

Community volunteers and BHS staff have coordinated the program with the schools and also served as guides: Camille Agricola, Ann Allen-Harper, Susan Atkinson, Lauren Bishop, Alice M. Bowsher, Laura Brown, Karen Brown, Alice M. Bowsher, Brenda Burrell, Carla Caldwell, Ehney Camp IV, Elizabeth Webb Collier, Kathy Courtland, Michelle Crunk, Claire-Louise Datnow, Julie and Christopher Dennis, Karyn Emison, Michelle Falls, Mary-Bester Grant, Joey Hester, Brenda Howell, Bill Jones, Leigh King, Jamie Lipsy, Edgar Marx, Jr., Norma Mauter, Gary McConnell, Beverly Miller, Cathy Muir, Barbara Pierce, Julie Roach, Nigel Roberts, Carole Sanders, Peggy Scott, Carol Slaughter, Marilyn Smith, Patricia Sprague, Barbara White, Marjorie White and Marjorie Lee White.

Ray Martin donated photography and production for *The Downtown Discovery Tour* video . Bettye Lee Hansen lent her marvelous voice. This video serves as pre-tour preparation.

In the late 1970s, curriculum specialist and volunteer Claire-Louise Datnow developed *DOWNTOWN-AN OUTDOOR CLASSROOM*, the background materials for teachers that accompany this tour are now found at www.bhistorical.com.

City of Birmingham school specialists, Lillie M. H. Fincher, Sadie Denson, and Donette Sparks, coordinated the Discovery Tour program with city schools, identifying special teachers to participate. Avondale, Bluff Park, Central Park, Cherokee Bend and Mountain Brook elementary and Advent Day schools have been long term supporters, especially teachers Prudie Felton, Janet Flakes, Louise McClery, Beverly Miller, Pat O'Donoghue, Peggy Scott and Mary Spain.

To our friends—the Birmingham Police and those who have welcomed student groups to Birmingham Realty Co., the Zinszer Bldg.–Spain & Gillon, L.L.C., the Peanut Depot, the Watts Bldg., and the banks AmSouth, Colonial, National Bank of Commerce, SouthTrust, and The Bank—multitudinous thanks for fixing up and sharing your special places.

*To all those who have helped others
discover downtown,we express deep gratitude.*

Rediscovering
Birmingham's Downtown
A History of the Tour

What glorious buildings Birmingham's city center had retained by the 1960s and 1970s. Such as they were: dirty, tired, old, dilapidated, and empty. One had to see them with eyes of love. They told the entire story of our city.

In 1976, the Birmingham Historical Society—with grants from the National Trust for Historic Preservation, the Junior League of Birmingham and the Linn-Henley Charitable Trust—formulated its DOWNTOWN DISCOVERY TOUR for school children. The program included a guided tour, a slide show (now a video), and teachers' handbooks and workshops. (Teacher materials are now on the web at www.bhistorical.org.)

In the 1970s, adults were not interested in GOING DOWNTOWN to look at old, rundown places. But children could see the beauty and the possibilities.

In the years that followed, enthusiastic volunteers led equally enthused students—principally third and fourth graders, but also occasionally adults—encouraging them to DISCOVER DOWNTOWN.

By the mid 1980s, the adults began buying up the old, tired buildings and fixing them up for new uses. The children cheered and wrote thank you letters as building after building was revived.

Today, local owners have restored and rehabbed hundreds of buildings. Entire districts within the city center thrive with new businesses. Cultural institutions have grown too. And many people live and work once again in the city center.

Bankers and lawyers, utility and insurance company employees, merchants, small business owners and government employees head to work here.

Now people who say they're going DOWNTOWN are probably headed to a museum or a festival, or to take a DOWNTOWN DISCOVERY TOUR to learn to look, to see and to appreciate the buildings and from whence they came . . . and the stories they have to tell.

It's a new century. Children who discovered DOWNTOWN as students now lead the tours and teach the children who take them, encouraging all to LOOK and SEE, ENJOY and CARE for our city's heritage.

The Birmingham Historical Society program, a pioneering effort in heritage education, has received national press and awards and continues to serve as a national model for efforts across America. The Discovery Tour begins its 25th year in 2002.

Defining Downtown

To generations, *downtown* was a magical place. . . full of bright lights and traffic . . . the place to linger a while, to shop or take in a movie.

Petula Clark's hit tune summed up the experience of *going downtown* in the 1960s, a time when downtowns across America were changing.

In the years following World War II, rapid construction of new suburban communities—accessed by new federally funded roads—expanded the limits of our nation's cities. New shopping centers and malls, and later office parks nearer the new homes, provided new shopping and entertainment. To get there, suburbanites drove cars, lots and lots and lots of them.

No longer did one have to go *downtown* to work, to shop or to be entertained.

No longer did streetcars, buses and trains provide superb public transit to and from the city center, as they had for nearly 100 years.

Downtown
Lyrics by Tony Hatch, as recorded by Petula Clark in 1964

When you're alone and life is making you lonely
you can always go—downtown.
When you got worries, all the noise and the hurry
Seems to help, I know—downtown.

Just listen to the music of the traffic in the city.
Linger on the sidewalks where the neon signs are pretty.
How can you lose?

The lights are much brighter there.
You can forget all your troubles, forget all your cares.
So go downtown, things'll be great when you're
Downtown—no finer place, for sure
Downtown—everything's waiting for you.

Don't hang around and let your problems surround you,
There are movie shows—downtown.
Maybe you know some little places to go to
where they never close—downtown.
Just listen to the rhythm of a gentle bossa nova.
You'll be dancing with him too before the night is over,
Happy again.

The lights are much brighter there.
You can forget all your troubles, forget all your cares.

So go downtown where all the lights are bright.
Downtown—waiting for you tonight.
Downtown—you're gonna be all right now.

And you may find somebody kind to help
and understand you.
Someone who is just like you and needs a gentle hand to
guide them along.

So maybe I'll see you there.
We can forget all our troubles, forget all our cares.
So go downtown, things'll be great when you're
Downtown—don't wait a minute more
Downtown—everything's waiting for you.

Downtown, downtown, downtown, downtown. . . .

British singer Petula Clark's Grammy-winning performance of *Downtown* helped her become the first English woman to hit the top of the American music charts. The Welbeck Music Ltd. Of London, England recording of this 1964 song has been re-released on CD as *Downtown: The Greatest Hits of Petula Clark*, BMG Distribution, Buddha Records 74446559671 2. Tony Hatch's 1964 lyrics are reprinted with the permission of MCA Music Publishing, a division of MCA, Inc., NY, NY.

Brief History of
Birmingham's Downtown

Just a little more than 125 years ago, Downtown Birmingham was a cornfield, surrounded by forests. In nearby hills lay rich deposits of coal, iron ore and limestone—the materials for making iron and steel.

In 1870, the track for two railroads was headed our way. At the point the lines crossed, someone would build a city at the center of the mineral region.

Southerners bought up the farmlands and planned a "magic little industrial city." They named it Birmingham, after the thriving English industrial center.

By the late 1880s, iron ores poured forth from Red Mountain mines and coal was mined from the Warrior and Cahaba fields. Sloss and many other furnaces made these minerals into pig iron. Foundries poured the iron to make pipe and stoves.

People flocked to the booming city from all over the Southern and Northern industrial centers of the United States and from foreign nations. Brick buildings—trimmed with "fancy details"—lined downtown streets. Birmingham was one of the largest cities in the South. Everyone called it "The Magic City."

At the turn of the 20th century, another boom began. Ten railroads laid track to the city center. Mines and mills continued to produce iron and steel. The skies were filled with soot, a welcome sign of prosperity.

Downtown emerged as the financial and service center for the industrial city. The barons of iron and steel, doctors, lawyers, bankers, businessmen, public officials, merchants and shopkeepers all had offices and stores downtown.

This was a Southern city, a city in black and white. Jim Crow laws maintained the separation of races into separate geographic districts. In the 1910s, Fourth Avenue developed as the black business district, with stores, services and theaters here catering to captive consumers.

Taking advantage of newly invented steel-frame construction, tall and elaborate "skyscrapers" rose on downtown street corners, drastically changing the skyline and providing work space for thousands of workers. Streetcars—a superb system of mass transit—got them here and back home. The city enjoyed the second (to Los Angeles) longest trackage in the nation.

The construction boom continued throughout the 1920s, with buildings becoming more and more elaborate. With the depression of the 1930s, "hard times came to Birmingham and stayed longest," as the local saying goes. There was little new construction for a long time.

During the 1960s, civil rights organizers staged boycotts and marches to downtown stores and City Hall protesting local segregation laws. In May of 1963, thousands of children joined the nonviolent marches, forcing the federal government to enact legislation guaranteeing freedom in public accommodations to all Americans. The national battle for civil rights was won on downtown Birmingham streets.

At the city's centennial in 1971, several office towers and the Civic Center complex rose. The landscaping of 20th Street reestablished 20th as the main axis and traditional heart of the city center. Later, trees lined all city center streets.

In the 1980s, historic preservation returned many buildings to new uses. Attractive new buildings complemented the old. Banks, utilities, cultural institutions and city-wide festivals grew. By the 1990s, enthusiastic urbanites also filled "lofty" living spaces.

Today, buildings of every period of our city's history line our streets. Unseen and unnoticed by the average person, they offer a fabulous record of Birmingham's growth.

With an alert eye, you can DISCOVER the stories they have to tell.

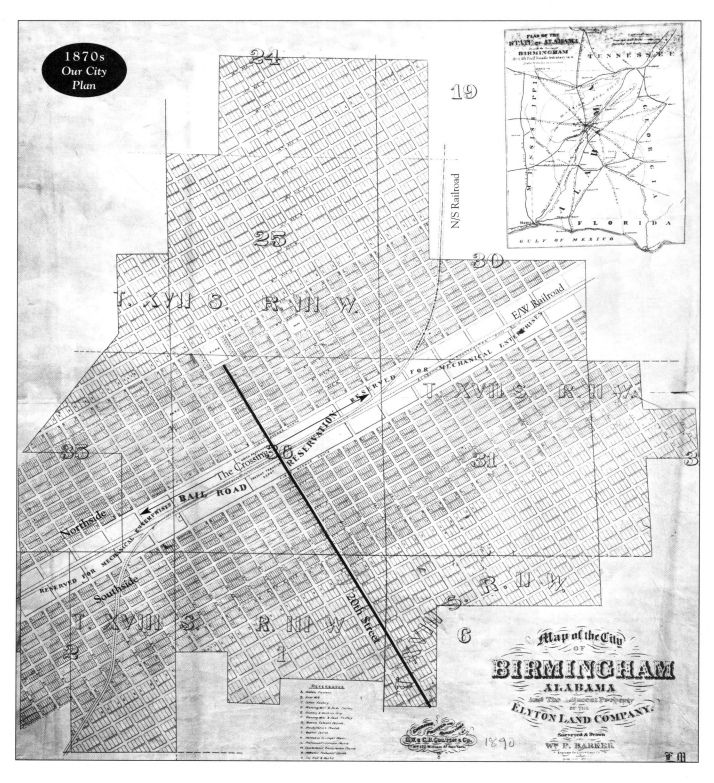

As this 1870s map shows, 20th Street—leading from Red Mountain across Southside (the south side of the tracks) and early industrial, business and residential districts to a central park—forms the spine of the city. At the core of the orderly streets and avenues are the reservations for railroads and industrial enterprises.

Founding the City
Our Historic Heart

John T. Milner
Railroad engineer
(1826-1898)

Most cities have a place where it all began.

Birmingham began at the crossing of two railroads. For a distance of 14 blocks, their tracks run parallel to one another. On either side of the tracks, railroad engineers laid out the lots and blocks, streets and avenues of our city on both the north and the south sides of the tracks.

Josiah Morris
Montgomery banker
(1818-1891)

City fathers had bought up the farmlands and forests. On these 4,150 acres, they planned Birmingham. At the core of their plan were the wide reservations for railroad and mechanical enterprises. To these reservations, they sought to attract industry to grow their speculative venture. They incorporated Birmingham on December 19, 1871.

Col. James R. Powell ran the company that founded Birmingham and also served as Mayor. A successful stagecoach operator, Powell had traveled extensively across Europe and visited British industrial centers. In his vision, Alabama's Birmingham centered within a great mineral region would become an industrial giant unlike other cities in the rural, agrarian South.

Col. James R. Powell
Planter/stagecoach operator
(1814-1876)

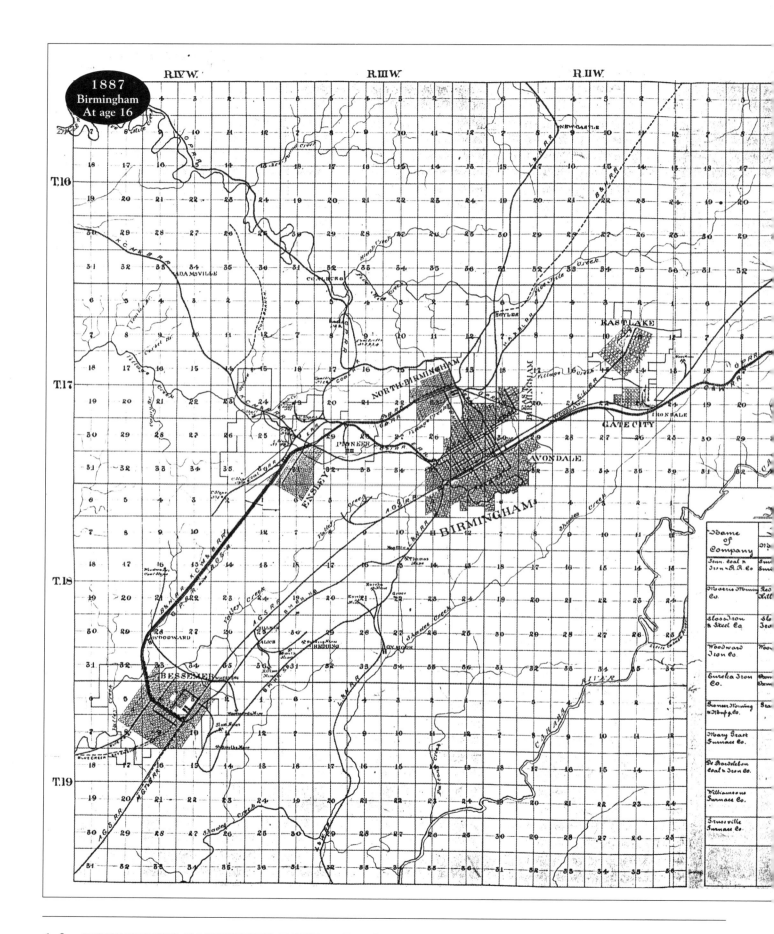

THE MINING, METALLURGIC AND INDUSTRIAL DISTRICT OF BIRMINGHAM ALA.

SCALE ¾ INCH = 1 MILE

by

Riccio, Sloan & Vedeler

CIVIL AND MINING ENGRS, ARCHTS.

BIRMINGHAM, ALA. P.O.B. 514

Note

▬▬▬ *Constructed Railways*

--- *proposed Railways*

ǂ *Furnace*

⤳ *Iron Ore Mine*

• *Coal Mine*

Magic Minerals

The rapid building of railroads, mines, and mills made Birmingham a city that grew like magic. During the 1880s, on sites superbly located with respect to minerals and transportation, 10 furnace companies began making iron.

Messrs. Riccio, Sloan and Vedeler made this map documenting the mineral region's amazing growth. They sited railways, furnaces, and iron ore and coal mines, noting their names and production.

Birmingham—the city at the center of the region—is the grid of streets and avenues at the hub of the surrounding industrial centers: Bessemer, Ensley, North Birmingham, East Birmingham, Avondale, East Lake, Gate City, Trussville and Leeds.

L&N Shed

L&N Station

Elyton Land Co.

1899
20th Street

Looking north on 20th Street

Andrew Fiorella's Blacksmithy

Twenty years after its founding, Birmingham was the main city of the Alabama mineral region. Its commercial core of offices and stores extended from the railroad tracks north to Third Avenue.

Horse-drawn wagons and streetcars transported people and goods through the early city's wide, dirt streets, keeping many a blacksmith busy shoeing horses.

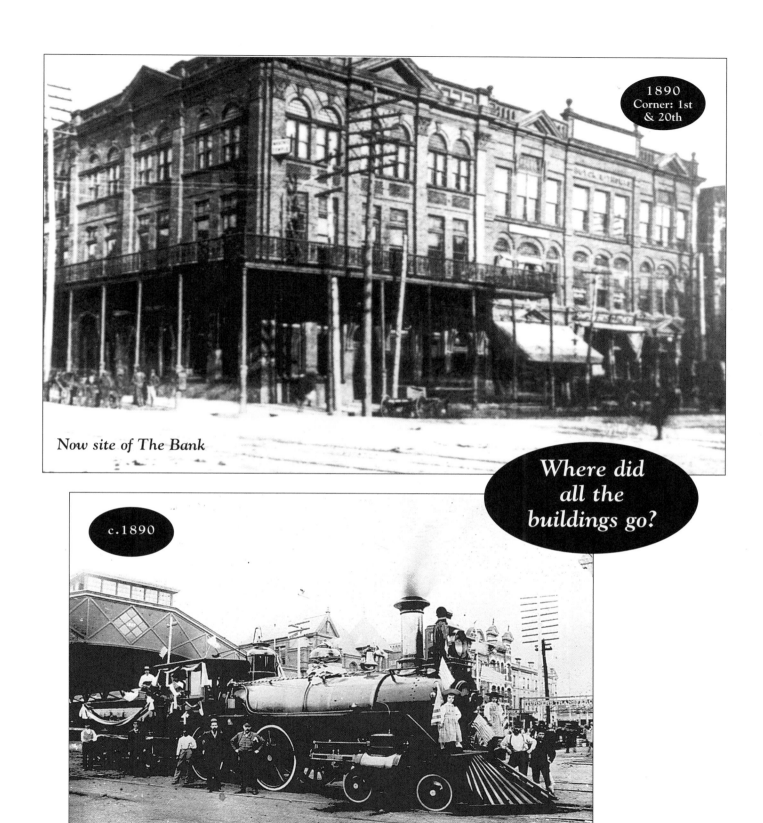

1890
Corner: 1st
& 20th

Now site of The Bank

c.1890

Where did
all the
buildings go?

Incoming trains brought new arrivals to the booming industrial city.

1898

L&N Station

L&N Shed

City life at the turn of the century centered upon the comings and goings at L&N Station. In this photograph well-wishers fill the train shed and 20th Street as they bid goodby to volunteers leaving to fight in the Spanish-American War. At this time, trains pulled straight into the shed to load and unload passengers.

Look carefully. The streetcar is electric!

1908
20th Street

Looking north from Second Avenue

By 1900, our out-of-nowhere Magic City had become Alabama's largest with a population of more than 38,000. In 1910, through consolidation with surrounding industrial suburbs, the City's population rose to 132,685. A proven producer of iron, cast iron pipe, and steel rail, Birmingham was the South's largest industrial workplace.

1913

Frank Nelson

Brown Marx

Empire

Heaviest Corner on Earth

Looking south on 20th Street

Skyscrapers, streetcars, power poles, and electric lights in this view of Birmingham's main street reflect the amenities of the fast growing, up-to-date urban center. City boosters called the intersection where four skyscrapers—including the Brown Marx and Empire buildings shown in this photograph—rose at the "Heaviest Corner on Earth."

**Where did the
station go?**

Accompanying Birmingham's population surge were increases
in every other indicator of prosperity: jobs, income, personal spend-
ing, home and office construction. The Birmingham city center
became a commercial, financial, and transportation center for the
region.

By 1910, nine railroads served Birmingham. Railroads carried
everything from thumb tacks to industrial equipment. In 1909, the
Southern Railroad built the buff brick Terminal Station with its
massive dome and towers. At the time this photograph was made,
98 passenger trains arrived and departed daily. The station served
as Birmingham's gateway to the world.

Courtesy ACIPCO

Blast furnace companies sold iron to foundries. The foundries remelted and poured it into molds to produce castings, including pipe, stoves and engines. With a steady supply of low-cost iron, Birmingham established itself as the center of cast-iron pipe manufacture in America.

Vulcan, Roman god of iron and smithing and Birmingham's symbol of its emerging iron and steel industry, was the state's exhibit at the St. Louis World's Fair in 1904.

1938 Sloss Furnaces

Blast Furnace No. 1

Casting Shed No. 1

Stack (to exhaust waste)

Stoves (heat air for the blast)

Skip Hoist (takes ore, coke & limestone)

Furnace No. 2

Casting Shed No. 2

Iron Ore

Coke

Limestone

Gondola car with iron bars

The Sloss Company built these furnaces to make iron, and money. Iron ore, coke and limestone delivered via rail are being loaded onto conveyors and transported via skip hoists into the two blast furnaces. Using these locally mined minerals, the furnaces produced iron bars used to make cast iron stoves, cotton gins, steel, and especially cast iron pipe. Sloss became America's largest producer of iron. Today, these furnaces, silent since 1970, are open to visitors, metal workers and festivals.

Phillips High

Comer

Watts

Buffalo Rock

Heaviest
Corner

20th Street

Retail District

Pizitz

Mortis Hotel

L & N
Station
& Shed

East

Railroad Reservation

West

Powell Ave.
Steam Plant

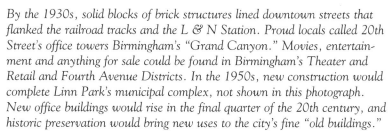

By the 1930s, solid blocks of brick structures lined downtown streets that flanked the railroad tracks and the L & N Station. Proud locals called 20th Street's office towers Birmingham's "Grand Canyon." Movies, entertainment and anything for sale could be found in Birmingham's Theater and Retail and Fourth Avenue Districts. In the 1950s, new construction would complete Linn Park's municipal complex, not shown in this photograph. New office buildings would rise in the final quarter of the 20th century, and historic preservation would bring new uses to the city's fine "old buildings."

This sketch of the city center, and of that same farmland purchased by the company that founded Birmingham in 1871, shows northside and southside (of the railraods), surrounding highways, and proposed new uses.

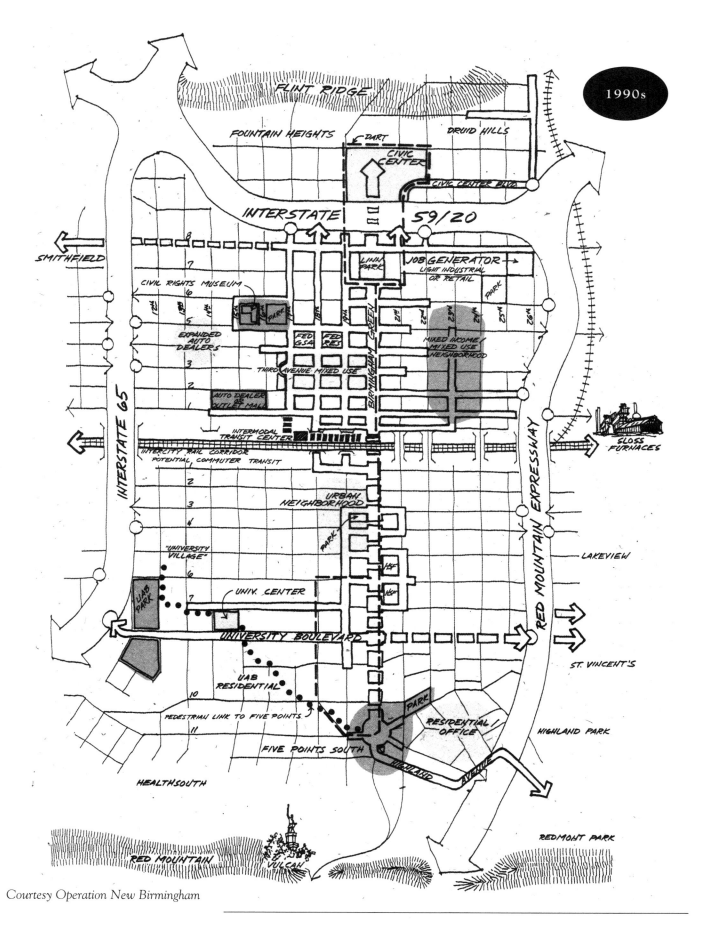

FLINT RIDGE

FOUNTAIN HEIGHTS   DART   DRUID HILLS

CIVIC CENTER

1990s

CIVIC CENTER BLVD.

INTERSTATE 59/20

SMITHFIELD

LINN PARK

JOB GENERATOR
LIGHT INDUSTRIAL OR RETAIL

PARK

CIVIL RIGHTS MUSEUM

EXPANDED AUTO DEALERS

PARK

FED GSA   FED RES

MIXED INCOME/ MIXED USE NEIGHBORHOOD

THIRD AVENUE MIXED USE

AUTO DEALER or OUTLET MALL

INTERSTATE 65

INTERMODAL TRANSIT CENTER

INTERCITY RAIL CORRIDOR
POTENTIAL COMMUTER TRANSIT

URBAN NEIGHBORHOOD

PARK

BIRMINGHAM GREEN

SLOSS FURNACES

RED MOUNTAIN EXPRESSWAY

LAKEVIEW

"UNIVERSITY VILLAGE"

UAB PARK

UNIV. CENTER

UNIVERSITY BOULEVARD

ST. VINCENT'S

UAB RESIDENTIAL

PEDESTRIAN LINK TO FIVE POINTS

PARK

RESIDENTIAL/ OFFICE

HIGHLAND PARK

FIVE POINTS SOUTH

HIGHLAND AVENUE

HEALTHSOUTH

REDMONT PARK

RED MOUNTAIN   VULCAN

Courtesy Operation New Birmingham

Birmingham Realty Company

Speculators & Their Magic Industrial City

In December 1870, ten men formed the Elyton Land Company. Their intent was to buy land and build a city at the center of the Alabama mineral region. They bought 4,150 acres and named the future city Birmingham after the world's largest industrial center: Birmingham, England.

James R. Powell became company president, as well as mayor and promoter of his dream for this "magic little industrial city." Birmingham would grow to become the South's largest industrial center.

ELYTON LAND COMPANY'S BUILDING.

Photographed in front of the Elyton Land Company's 20th Street offices are the men who bought the land, laid out the streets and avenues, brought in industries, and got the city rolling.

Both the name "Elyton" and the company remain today. Elyton is the residential neighborhood surrounding the Arlington Antebellum Home & Gardens.

1905
Newly built

Balustrade

Arch

Stained glass window

Iron grill

BIRMINGHAM REALTY COMPANY

The Elyton Land Company changed its name to Birmingham Realty Company and built these offices that remain today. It also took good care of its building.

2000
Well preserved

BIRMINGHAM REALTY COMPANY.

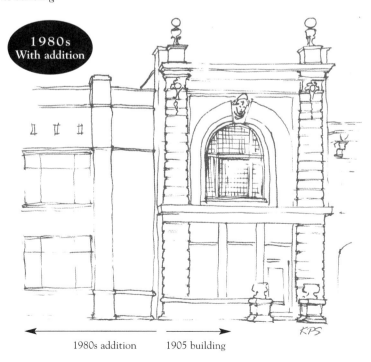

1980s
With addition

1980s addition   1905 building

I SPY
Awake Visual Awareness

History is where you find it. An important record lines our streets. Unseen and unnoticed, buildings offer fascinating visual records.

Find things that remain the same.

Most people see little of their immediate environment. Whether out of habit or preoccupation, we see only a fraction of that at which we look. By training our eyes to see in detail, our world grows in interest and quality.

A Borrowed Air of Authority
A Classical Details Hunt

Art historians describe the style of the Birmingham Realty Building as *Classical Revival*. Its designer found inspiration in the buildings of the Greeks and Romans. In 1905, all things *classical* were popular. So was a certain Roman smith who could make everything, as could area industries in this era.

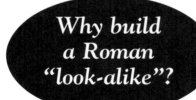

Why build a Roman "look-alike"?

Cartouche representing a Roman messenger set in a keystone

Cartouche or human face

Keystone—the central stone at the top of an arch

Egg-and-dart molding—an egg-shaped ornament alternating with a dart-like ornament

Dentils—a series of closely shaped ornamental blocks resembling teeth

Greek key molding—which must resemble ancient keys

Brass lion, the king of beasts!

Acanthus—a common plant of the Mediterranean region whose leaves often appear in ornament

Find these classical details.

Selling the City-Block By Block

Teller cage with decorative ironwork.

Inside, the company offices looks much like they did at the opening in 1905. A dramatic sky-lit chamber welcomes and impresses visitors. Then, patrons walked up to the teller windows and purchased land upon which they built homes and offices and industrial plants.

Along the walls hang the maps showing the land that the company divided into building lots and sold: the Birmingham city center, Highland Avenue, Norwood Boulevard, Chestnut Hills and Forest Park.

A REALTY company deals with REALTY. It buys, sells and develops land, buildings, and our city.

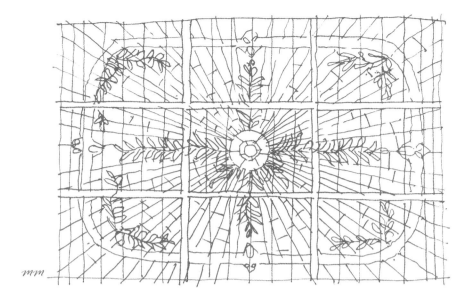

Stained glass

← Console bracket with
curled acanthus leaves

Coffered ceiling with plaster ornament

Wooden Balastrade

A golden light enters the interior through the open, second-story gallery. Stained
glass found extensive use in office and church windows in the early 20th century.

Steiner Building

Banking on Birmingham-Steiner Brothers & Their Building

Carl Steiner, left, receiving customers in the Steiner Brothers Banking Chambers, 2101 First Avenue North. Courtesy Arnold Steiner.

Burghard Steiner (1857-1923)   *Sigfried Steiner (1859-1902)*

Three generations of Steiner brothers ran Steiner Bank. Burghard and Siegfried Steiner came to Alabama from Bohemia, now part of the Czech Republic. In 1888, they opened an investment bank, convincing people worldwide to invest in and help Birmingham and Alabama grow. The brothers later moved their international banking business to New York City.

Their cousins Carl and Leo Steiner—and later Carl and Leo's grandsons Arnold and Bernard Steiner—ran Steiner Bank as a commercial bank, offering customers savings and checking accounts, loans and friendly, personal service.

Banking House & Gentlemen's Office

OLD BUILDINGS

Our city's oldest office buildings are
2 to 4–STORIES TALL
BUILT OF BRICK with
LOTS OF FANCY DETAIL.

In 1890, Steiner Brothers built
this robust brick and stone bank.

Are these the same building?

Commercial Bank

Offices for architects and investment bankers

HOW OLD BUILDINGS STAND UP

Old buildings have strong outside walls. The walls carry the floors. The people inside the building stand on the floors. This weight goes back into the wall. (A weight is also called a load.)

The strong outside walls are called LOAD BEARING WALLS. Load bearing walls are made of materials like stone and brick.

Outside
Looking at the building face

Inside
Taking off the building face

What it feels like!

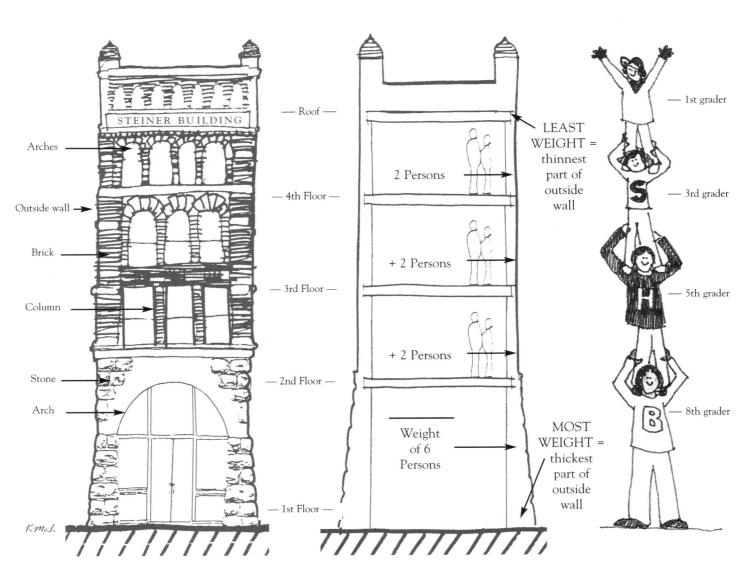

Outside labels:
Arches
Outside wall →
Brick
Column
Stone
Arch

STEINER BUILDING

— Roof —
— 4th Floor —
— 3rd Floor —
— 2nd Floor —
— 1st Floor —

KMcL

Inside labels:
2 Persons
+ 2 Persons
+ 2 Persons
Weight of 6 Persons

LEAST WEIGHT = thinnest part of outside wall

MOST WEIGHT = thickest part of outside wall

What it feels like labels:
— 1st grader
— 3rd grader
— 5th grader
— 8th grader

STANDING UP

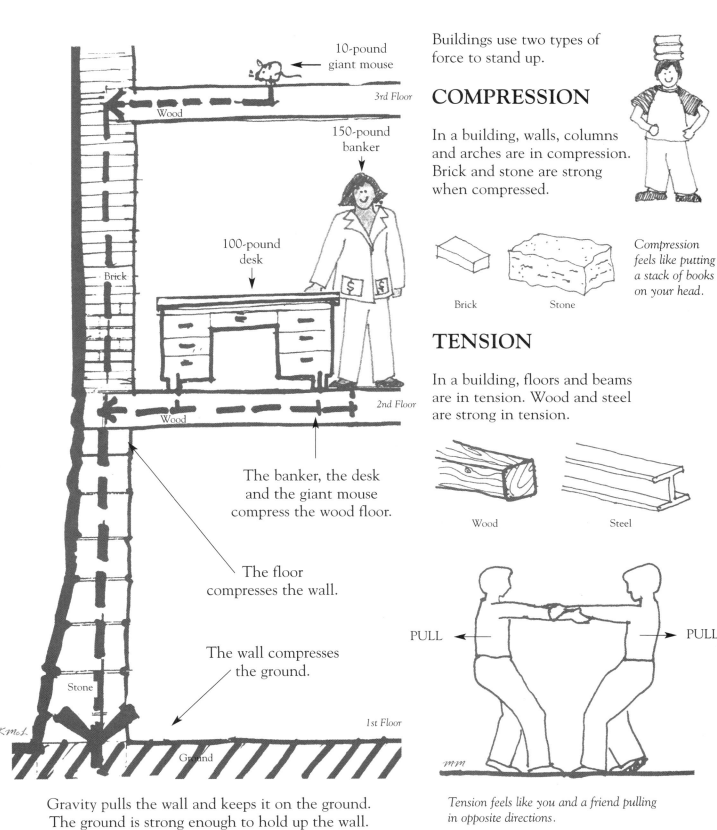

10-pound giant mouse

3rd Floor

Wood

150-pound banker

100-pound desk

Brick

2nd Floor

Wood

The banker, the desk and the giant mouse compress the wood floor.

The floor compresses the wall.

The wall compresses the ground.

Stone

1st Floor

Ground

Gravity pulls the wall and keeps it on the ground. The ground is strong enough to hold up the wall.

Buildings use two types of force to stand up.

COMPRESSION

In a building, walls, columns and arches are in compression. Brick and stone are strong when compressed.

Brick   Stone

Compression feels like putting a stack of books on your head.

TENSION

In a building, floors and beams are in tension. Wood and steel are strong in tension.

Wood   Steel

PULL   PULL

Tension feels like you and a friend pulling in opposite directions.

Florentine Building

In Love with His Teacher—Mr. Sims & Miss Hannah

A prominent lawyer is said to have built the Florentine Building to impress his art teacher, Miss Hannah Elliott. He wanted to marry her. The building's ornament recalls Italian palaces he and Miss Hannah's other students had visited on their grand European study tours and suggests a life they might enjoy together!

Miss Hannah Elliott (1876-1951), artist, teacher and spinster, worked unceasingly to establish an art museum for our city.

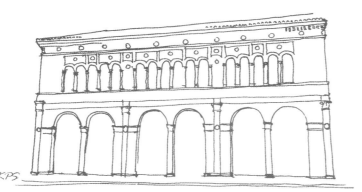

KPS

Did she marry him?

1928

A Gift to the Street
Terra Cotta
Treasure Hunt

Terra cotta—literally defined as *cooked earth*—is a fine-grained, brown-red clay that is most often fired to make flower pots and roof tiles. Pre-cast in blocks, *glazed* terra cotta becomes a *decorative* skin for buildings. This cladding provides sumptuous ornament and fireproofing.

Birmingham architects of the early 20th century specified glazed terra cotta for dozens of city center buildings. The Florentine Building is a spectacular showcase.

Here acanthus, potted in an urn, grows like a giant bean stalk up the building forming swirls just below the roof.

His & her cameos

Cherub in acanthus swirls

Cherubs with shield

Eagle within laurel wreath

Column capital with acanthus leaves & flower

Mom and Pop Stores
Family Enterprises

Wehby's fruit stand, Khattlar Wehby, proprietor

Sharbel's Arabic Market

Across from the Zinszer Building are two *Old Buildings*—both two-stories tall, built of brick with lots of fancy details. Their walls are load-bearing. These buildings are typical of 18th and 19th century small-town stores.

Typically, they housed mom-and-pop businesses on the street level. The store owners and their families resided upstairs. All family members worked together in the store.

Zinszer Building

Peter & Rosa's Palace–Recycled & Reused

Peter and Rosa Zinszer moved to Birmingham in 1884. The young couple opened a store which offered every possible home furnishing and several new services: "easy payment," an early version of credit, and home delivery. Zinszer's Mammoth Furniture House also advertised in the city's English and German language newspapers. Five years later, the highly successful store occupied this immense (for the era) cast-iron front store.

Rosa Zinszer (1858-1930)

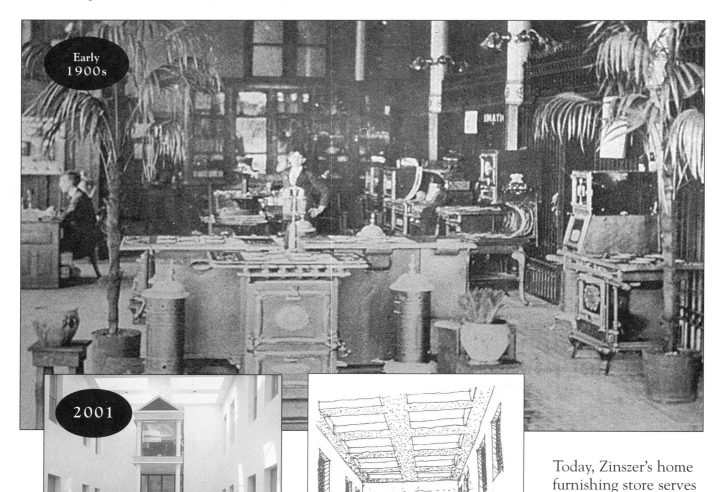

Early 1900s

2001

Today, Zinszer's home furnishing store serves as offices for lawyers. The central atrium space is skylit and surrounded by interior windows which permit entry of natural light to offices within.

1978

Before: Tired old building

Zinszer Building Then & Now
A Cinderella Story

When this photograph was made, the Zinszer store's cast-iron front was corroded, its paint peeled and the roof leaked. A new owner restored the cast iron—molding new pieces from remaining ones—and converting the store to offices.

1985

After: Landmark once again

Mass-produced Strength & Glitz
THE CAST IRON HUNT

As urban areas expanded following the Civil War, businessmen chose cast-iron fronted premises, offering their services from buildings clothed in the architectural style of Italian merchant princes. In some American cities, whole districts of cast-iron buildings were built.

Iron fronts could be mass-produced cheaply and prefabricated in hundreds of separate pieces as large as a column or as small as a flower. The pieces were molded, polished and tested for fit before final assembly. At the site, craftsmen bolted the iron pieces together, attaching them to the building that had been constructed to receive them.

The prefabricated fronts could be molded to a variety of forms and richly decorated in a style known as *Italianate*, an exuberant American version of Italian Renaissance palaces.

The ornate fronts were practical for another reason. The strength of a metal-supported facade provides a structural solution impossible with traditional brick construction supporting the weight of walls and roof. Such a front also allows for larger expanses of glass, permitting light to pour into interior spaces.

Columns

Find these cast-iron details.

Column capitals with acanthus leaves and rosettes (the flowers)

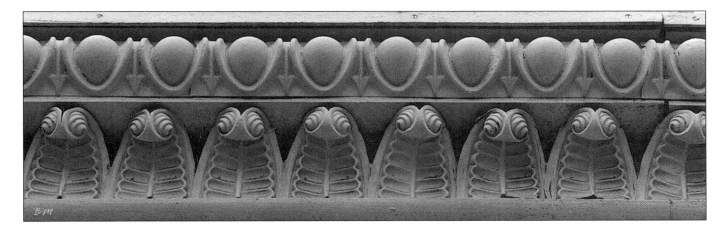

Egg-and-dart and acanthus moldings

1913
Under
costruction

Steel frame

Terra cotta cladding

1st Methodist

Residential district

First
Presbyterian

The Tutwiler

21st Street

F. W. MARK CONSTRUCTION COMPANY INC
GENERAL CONTRACTORS

AM ALABAMA

JEFFERSON COUNTY SAVINGS BANK BLDG
BIRMINGHAM - ALA - JULY-25-1913

Second Avenue North

Jefferson County Savings Bank–Comer Building

Immigrant Makes It Big Time–Mr. Enslen & His Bank

Construction crew at the old Tutwiler Hotel on 20th Street

Christian Enslen immigrated from Germany in 1845 and learned the blacksmith trade. While his son Eugene was a child, he served the Confederacy by turning out thousands of horseshoes for the calvary. Father and son came to early Birmingham and opened a store. It prospered and, by 1885, provided funds to start a bank. The family bank also prospered. Christian served as president and Eugene as cashier. By 1913, with Eugene Enslen as president, the bank built this distinguished office tower known for years as the Jefferson County Savings Bank, Comer Building, and later City Federal.

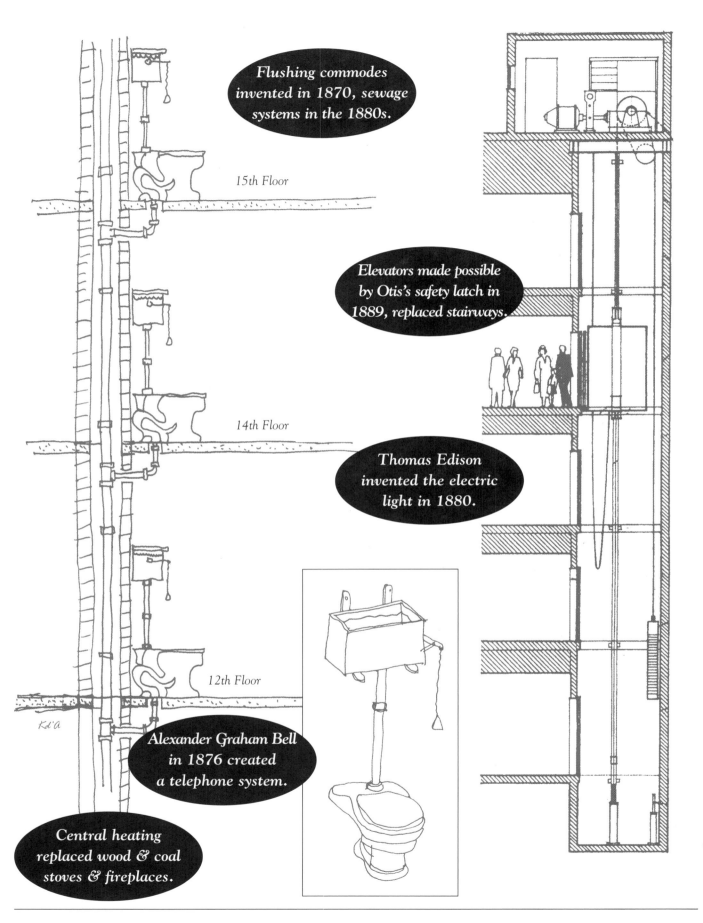

Flushing commodes invented in 1870, sewage systems in the 1880s.

15th Floor

Elevators made possible by Otis's safety latch in 1889, replaced stairways.

14th Floor

Thomas Edison invented the electric light in 1880.

12th Floor

Kd'A

Alexander Graham Bell in 1876 created a telephone system.

Central heating replaced wood & coal stoves & fireplaces.

Scraping The Sky–The Office Tower

Birmingham's first skyscraper rose in 1901 and was quickly followed by 12 more high-rises before World War I. An efficient system of mass transportation—a streetcar network linking the city center to other industrial centers and the suburbs—carried large numbers of workers downtown to their jobs in these giant towers.

New technologies permitted the rise of *skyscraper office buildings* in the late 19th century. Steel columns and beams carried the weight of the giant buildings, and allowed for larger windows and open arrangements of space. Walls no longer needed to be load bearing.

Bank president Eugene Enslen places the bolt of the first steel column, April 13, 1913.

Steel is a very strong building material. Architects use it to make up the skeleton of skyscrapers. Steel columns and steel beams support floors and ceilings.

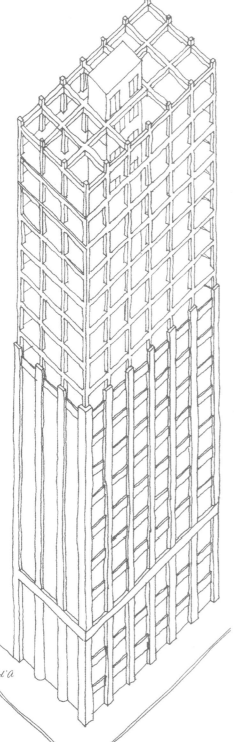

A building's bones, its steel frame, hold the building up.

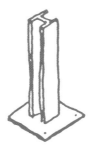

My bones, a skeleton costume

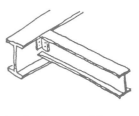

Steel columns and beams

Educating Farmers
Professor Massey's School & Building

Richard Massey arrived in Birmingham in 1887 with little more than his lunch and a letter of introduction. He rented a typewriter and a room, enrolled students and began teaching them business skills. People from rural areas were pouring into the city. They needed new skills to take advantage of new job opportunities.

Massey developed a network of business colleges throughout the southeast. His Birmingham college served as their architectural model. Across the street from it, he built the Massey Building, a 10-story office tower.

Terra cotta flourishes on the Massey Building include Massey's coat of arms, showing a knight's armor with shield, feathered helmet and the initial "M."

Professor Massey's business school taught by doing. Students learned business skills by participating in real life activities. To learn typing, they typed. Graduates achieved positions as bookkeepers, secretaries and managers.

THE FANCY BRICKWORK HUNT
2000 Block Third Avenue North

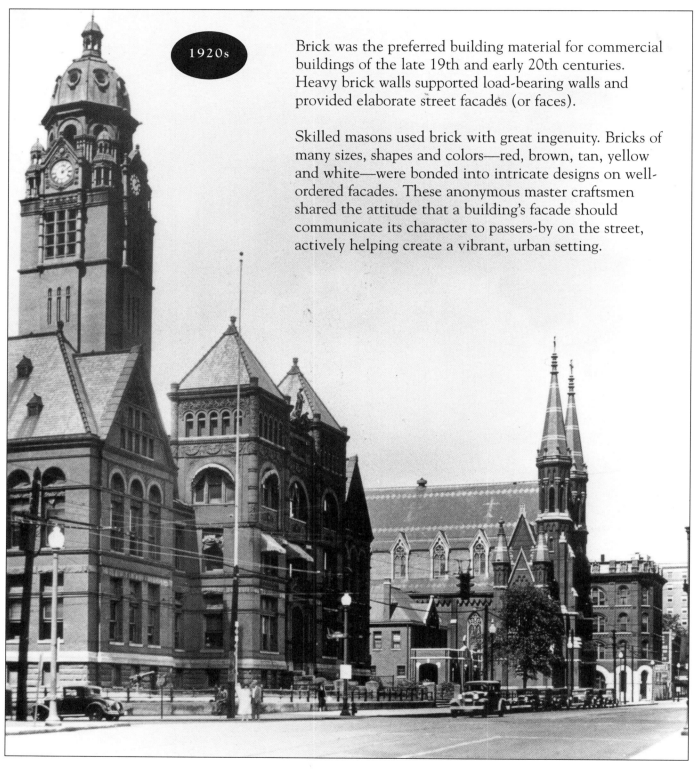

1920s

Brick was the preferred building material for commercial buildings of the late 19th and early 20th centuries. Heavy brick walls supported load-bearing walls and provided elaborate street facades (or faces).

Skilled masons used brick with great ingenuity. Bricks of many sizes, shapes and colors—red, brown, tan, yellow and white—were bonded into intricate designs on well-ordered facades. These anonymous master craftsmen shared the attitude that a building's facade should communicate its character to passers-by on the street, actively helping create a vibrant, urban setting.

Jefferson County's 19th century Courthouse (site of today's Concord Center) & St. Paul's Catholic Cathedral boast some of the city's finest brickwork.

In the 19th century, masons used many shapes and patterns of brick to enliven their designs.

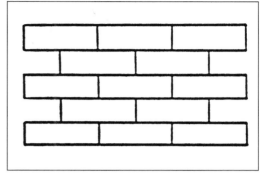

Stretcher Bond

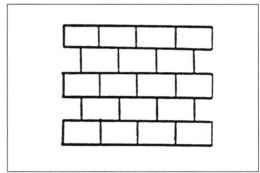

Header Bond

Find these brick in the 2000 Block of Third.

A header is the end of a brick.

A stretcher is the long side of a brick.

Bonding patterns are achieved by alternating stretchers and headers. This is done for strength and durability.

SouthTrust Building
A Place to be Trusted

When this marble palace opened in 1922, the bankers who built it considered the bank building "a symbol and a sign that the place and the men who handle its money are something more than a mere business. That within its walls, honor and fidelity and a high sense of the sacredness and dignity of being trusted, have an abiding place."

The bank looks like a Roman temple, outside and within. Its 20th Street front features white marble from a newly opened vein at Gantt's Quarry in Sylacauga, Alabama. This vein would also supply many public buildings in Washington D. C.

Wouldn't you TRUST this bank?

Originally, an eagle crowned great bronze doors at the 20th Street entrance, helping create the impression that this bank is a well defended place.

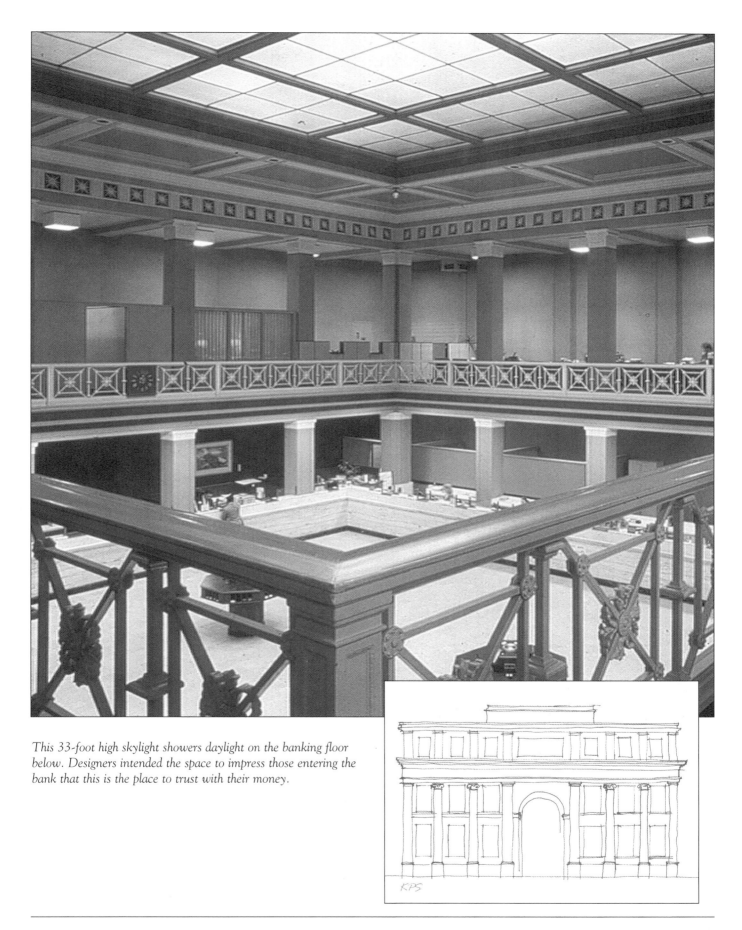

This 33-foot high skylight showers daylight on the banking floor below. Designers intended the space to impress those entering the bank that this is the place to trust with their money.

KPS

Heaviest Corner on Earth
Headquarters for the Industrial Giants

1913

Red Mountain · The Bank · Woodward-NBC · Empire · Brown Marx · Brown Marx · 20th St. · Caldwell-Milner · McAdory · 1st Ave. · 20th St. · SAKS · BTNB · TUXEDO

In an amazingly short time, Birmingham's urban look changed from outpost town to that of a booming city. By 1912, all four corners of the First Avenue and 20th Street intersection were occupied by office towers. Proud citizens touted the intersection as the "Heaviest Corner on Earth." The skies were filled with soot, a welcome sign of prosperity.

Empire
Colonial
Bank

Brown
Alden

The
Bank

Woodward-
NBC

PORTERS

WESTERN
UNION

By the early 1920s, when this photograph of First Avenue looking east
was made, streetcars were vying for space with an ever-expanding number
of automobiles. First Avenue North was a major east-west thoroughfare.

1909

Birmingham's skyline climbs to 16 stories as this office tower rises. Posing for this photograph are teams of expert craftsmen, who mortar and anchor the exterior terra cotta block to form the building face.

The Empire Building

Busts of Roman and British emperors, rendered in terra cotta blocks, crown arches at the top of the Empire-Colonial Bank Building.

Locals call these arches the hall of fame, identifying the busts as those who designed and built the splendid building.

William Welton, the young architect pictured in his library with his draftsman (a helper who draws plans and sketches), designed the tower, including each terra cotta block.

Welton had studied architecture at M. I. T. and in Paris, and interned with the New York-based McKim, Meade & White, one of America's finest firms.

THE CORNICE HUNT
1st & 20th–The Crowning Glory

Early 20th century skyscrapers resemble large columns. Columns have a base, shaft and capital. So do these skyscrapers. However, the skyscraper base is 2 to 3 stories, its shaft is 10 to 12 stories and its CORNICE 2 to 3 stories.

A cornice is the projecting, ornament molding along the top of a building. Carved of stone or molded of copper or terra cotta, a building cornice is like an old-fashioned lady's bonnet, visually the crown.

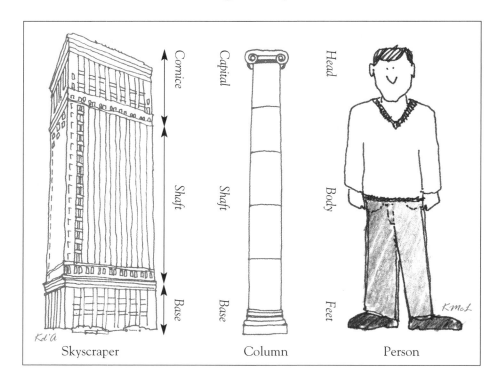

Skyscraper — Column — Person

Cornice, Empire-Colonial Bank Building

Find these cornices.

Cornice, The Bank

Morris Avenue

Getting the Goods In & Out

1910s

Early 1930s

1910

Trains brought goods to Morris Avenue where they were sold in bulk. With horse-and-buggies and later trucks and vans, merchants picked up the goods and resold them in stores across the city.

Brick warehouses held the bulk goods during processing and refining. Refining included roasting, as in peanuts and coffee. Peanut Depot roasters have been operating continuously since 1917.

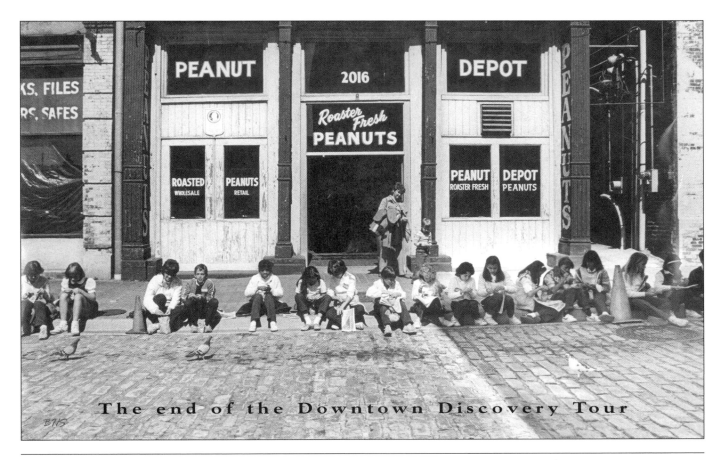

The end of the Downtown Discovery Tour

DOWNTOWN DISCOVERY TOUR
Glossary

Arcade: a range of arches carried on piers or columns

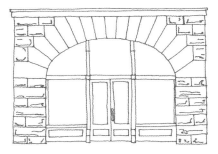

Arch: a curved structure over an open space

Architect: a person who designs and oversees the construction of buildings

Architecture: the profession of designing buildings and other structures

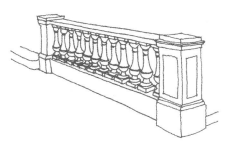

Balustrade: a series of short posts or pillars that support a rail

Beam: a horizontal structural member carrying a load

Brass: metal alloy (resembling gold when polished) consisting of copper and zinc

Brick: a block of clay dried in sun or kiln; a building material

Cast Iron: molten iron molded to a desired shape

Cherub: an angel represented as a winged child, often with a chubby innocent face

Column: a rounded support that holds up a building or structure; composed of base, shaft and capital.

Concrete: a man-made stone-like building material

Cornice: the exterior trim at the very top of a building; the Greek work for crown

Demolish: to tear down or estroy

Dentils: a series of rectangular blocks arranged like teeth

Department Store: a large store divided into different departments of merchandise

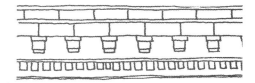

Egg-and-Dart: an oval molding made up of alternating egg-shaped and dart-shaped elements

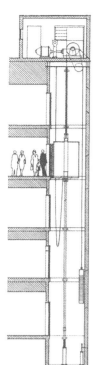

Elevator: a moving platform or cage for carrying people from one level to another in a building; invented by Elisha Otis in 1853

Elyton Land Company: Birmingham's first real estate company, the company that acquired the land where Birmingham's city center is located today

Facade: the front of a building

Flushing Commode: old-fashioned toilet, into which a lever releases water stored above the toilet to flush the toilet bowl

Furnace: a structure for generating heat to warm homes and buildings; a structure to smelt coal, iron ore and limestone into iron

Garden: a piece of land used to grow flowers and shrubs to decorate land

Greek Key: an ornament consisting of repeated angular figures formed by interlocking vertical and horizontal bands

Grid Plan: a system of reference lines intersecting at right angles, used to map an area

Keystone: the central stone of an arch

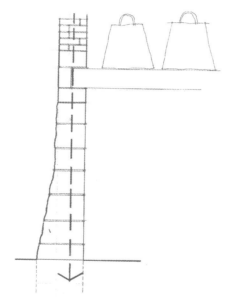

Load Bearing: walls that hold up the weight of floors

Magic City: nickname given to Birmingham, during the late 19th century to attest to its rapid growth as the South's largest industrial center

Modillion: a scroll shaped bracket used in a series, often under a cornice

Mom & Pop Store: a small, family owned and run business

Municipal Building: city government building or office

Museum: a building where works of art are displayed and stored

Old Building: building constructed before the invention of structural-steel and indoor plumbing; typically 2-4 stories tall, made of brick and lots of fancy detail

Pediment: a triangular or round shape used over a door or window for decoration

Paver: brick, stone or flat concrete slab used to make roads and sidewalks

Pig Iron: iron tapped from a blast furnace

Preservation: to keep in existence; to make lasting; to preserve

Recycle: to adapt for reuse; to use again in original form with minimal alteration

Restoration: to return a building to the way it was, usually to the time of its construction

Renovation: to fix up a building

Roaster: an oven used to heat and cook by exposure to dry heat

Saloon: a bar

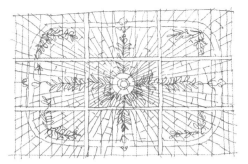

Stained Glass: small glass panes of many colors arranged into decorative patterns or pictures

Steel: refined pig iron, possessing qualities of strength

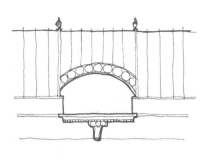

Teller Cage: bars behind which a bank teller stands

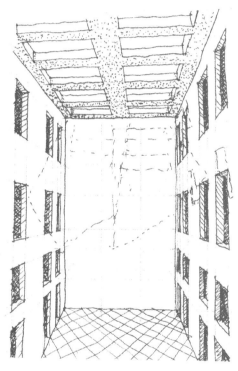

Skylight: glass window in the ceiling of a building

Skyscraper: a building of at least 10 stories built only after the invention of elevators, steel framing and flushing commodes

Glossary Drawings by Michelle Morgan, unless otherwise noted, text by Edgar Marx, Jr.

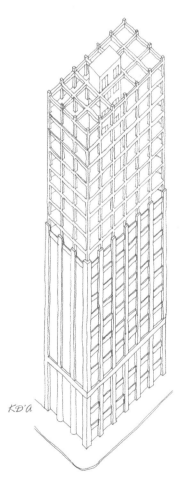

Steel Frame: the steel skeleton of a building

Stone: hard substance formed of mineral matter or rock

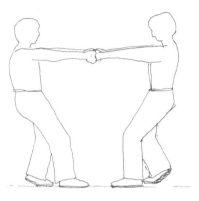

Tension: the act of straining; a device for maintaining stress

Terra Cotta: clay baked to use as exterior building decoration

Warehouse: a building to store goods

BIRMINGHAM HISTORICAL SOCIETY

Linn Park

HISTORY HUNT

THE 20TH STREET PARK & GOVERNMENTAL CENTER

The Park on 20th Street

Birmingham's founders planned a single park.

The first city plan shows the park as an open green space a block and a half long. Central Park sits at the head of 20th Street, the city's spine, leading from Red Mountain across Southside, the railroad tracks, and the future business district.

City fathers hoped Birmingham would become the state capital. Henry Wellege of Milwaukee published a drawing showing the park with an open, elevated space surrounded by houses and virgin trees. Note the young trees recently planted along the park's edges and the building intended to house our state government.

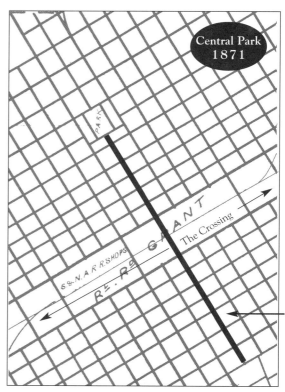

Capitol Park
1900

Woodrow
Wilson Park
1919

Grounds for Pleasure and Play

In 1900, parks were considered pleasure grounds and splices of the country within the city. The photograph above shows a gentleman posing in front of the iron fountain at the center of the park. Benches offer park visitors views of the surrounding houses and trees. The trees have grown in the 15 years since the Henry Wellege view.

Nearly 20 years later, the park has a new name, that of Woodrow Wilson, the United States President who led the nation through World War I. Well-traveled dirt paths indicate lots of park users, especially neighborhood children, playing with hoops. Trees provide shade.

In the early 20th century, every city worth its salt built a civic center, a monumental space surrounded by fine public buildings in the classical style. Shortly after World War I, public-spirited Birmingham citizens hoped to create such a City Beautiful amenity here. Their plan locates new civic buildings and honors military heroes.

In the 1919 plan, the park becomes an open plaza terminating the 20th Street axis with an impressive memorial: a 250-foot tall Tower of Progress. This obelisk, as high as a 25-story building, honors the sacrifices of American veterans.

Flanking the proposed tower are new city hall and county courthouse buildings. Other major public and private buildings surround the park, which is extended a block further south to Sixth Avenue.

The Place to Honor Heroes

Find these monuments.

Find the heroes by drawing lines to link the monument to the persons remembered.

Monument	People It Remembers
Flame	Confederate soldiers and sailors
Obelisk	George Washington
Rock	Revolutionary War patriots
Seated lady	Spanish American War soldiers
Soldier holding musket	World War I soldiers
Soldier with an arm raised	Teacher Mary Cahalan
Statue	Thomas Jefferson (for whom our county is named)
	Veterans of all wars

Birmingham's Civic Center

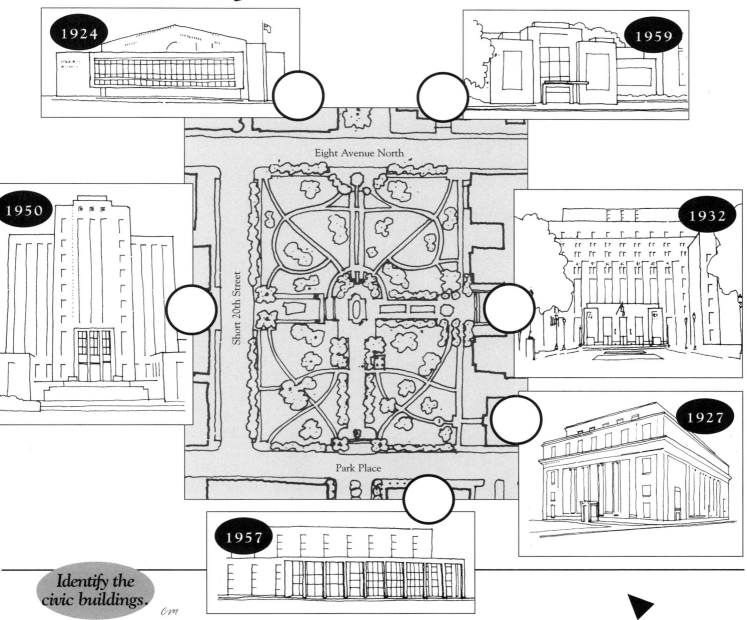

Eight Avenue North

Short 20th Street

Park Place

1924
1959
1950
1932
1927
1957

Identify the civic buildings. cm

Identify the civic buildings by placing their numbers ▼ *in the location (◯) on the map above.*

1. Birmingham Board of Education
2. Birmingham City Hall
3. Birmingham Museum of Art
4. Birmingham Public Library
5. Boutwell Auditorium
6. Jefferson County Courthouse

How long did it take to complete Birmingham's Civic Center? From 1919 to 19__ __ or _____ years.

Compare what was built with what was planned in the 1919 drawing.

What was built as planned? _____

Great Civic Space and Outdoor Living Room

Jefferson County Courthouse

Paths & Pools 1933

Birmingham City Hall

Construction in the 1930s provided formal paths, pools and a new central axis. An ornamental pool marks the center of the park and the intersection of two major walkways that divide the park into four sections. Reflecting pools extend from the center, visually linking city hall and the courthouse.

Park Features and Furnishings

Check features you observe.

NATURAL
- __ botanical gardens
- __ lawns
- __ lines of trees
- __ rose gardens
- __ special plantings
- __ trees:
  - __ oak
  - __ hickory
  - __ poplar
- __ zoological gardens

MAN-MADE
- __ axis linking city hall and the courthouse
- __ baseball diamond
- __ basketball court
- __ benches
- __ broad steps
- __ dirt bike trails
- __ fountain
- __ gazebo
- __ golf links
- __ hiking trails
- __ monuments
- __ paths
- __ pools
- __ roads
- __ runnel or cascade of water
- __ service building
- __ sidewalks
- __ statues
- __ swimming pools
- __ swings and slides
- __ tables and chairs
- __ trash receptacles
- __ walls of _____

Features are: __ orderly   __ haphazard

Renovations in the 1980s made the park a lively and welcoming space. A new fountain shoots forth at the center. Pavements are patterned. Benches, tables and chairs encourage nearby office workers to take a break in the park.

Linn Park 1985

Check uses you observe.

- __ eating
- __ event-attending
- __ exploring
- __ history hunting
- __ hanging out
- __ jogging
- __ listening to music
- __ picnicking
- __ playing
- __ playing ball
- __ playing cards
- __ reading
- __ relaxing
- __ sitting
- __ skateboarding
- __ sleeping
- __ sunbathing
- __ talking
- __ wading
- __ walking

What are most people doing?

_____

What uses are prohibited?

_____

Jefferson County Courthouse

Courthouse ornament tells Alabama history. A photographer took these views in the sculptor's studio before the panels were installed on the courthouse.

Find the panels.

1. Indian 10,000 B. C.
Native Americans called the future state of Alabama home. These hunter-gatherers later grew corn but did not live in tepees.

2. Spanish 1540
Hernando de Soto claimed Alabama for Spain and the Catholic Church.

3. French 1682
French explorer Robert de LaSalle traveled down the Mississippi River and claimed its watershed for France. The fleur-de-lis symbolizes France.

4. English 1763
The Treaty of Paris ceded Florida and Louisiana to the English King George III.
1802
England also claimed Alabama as part of the English-governed state of Georgia.

5. Coming of the White Man 1814
After the Creek Indian War, white and African American pioneers began settling Jefferson County. Most came in wagons from the Eastern seaboard and its ports.

6. American 1819
Alabama became a state of the United States of America, shown here by the coat of arms of the 13 American colonies and the scales of justice.

7. Confederate 1861-1865
Alabama joined the Confederate States of America, with Montgomery serving as the first Confederate capital.

Outside the Courthouse

Find these panels.

These panels show how citizens breaking the law will be treated.

With "Justice"

With "Mercy"

Patriotic themes — especially our national bird, the eagle — provide other courthouse ornament.

Searching the outside of the courthouse, how many eagles can you find?

Search for eagles.

5	Keep going.
7	You've found a lot, but there are more.
9	You're getting closer.
35	You're just guessing.

Did you find several blind owls?

When the courthouse was built, people thought that Alabama was a Muskogee Indian word meaning "Here we rest." Scholars now think Alabama is the Choctaw word for "thicket clearers," those who clear the land of dense brush before the raising of crops can begin.

Inside the Courthouse

The courthouse contains courtrooms and offices for services such as driver's and marriage licenses, and for county officials and agencies. These murals in the entrance lobby tell stories of the Old and New South.

1929

The Old South

The economy of the Old South is based
on the cultivation of land.

Looking from bottom to top, find the field hands picking cotton and cutting cane which steamboats transport to markets in the north and Europe, thereby providing a luxurious lifestyle for the enormous feminine figure. Find the slave cottages and the cotton warehouse on the docks, left, and a master's white-columned main house, right.

O cane cutters O cotton pickers O slave cottages

O masters at play O cotton warehouse

O docks with steamboat O plantation main house

Who works? _____ Who plays?_____

The New South

The economy of the New South is based
on industrial production.

Looking from bottom to top, on the left, find the furnace workers. They are "rodding the hole," forcing a rod into the fiery furnace to insure that the 3,500 degree iron can freely exit the furnace. Right, a coal miner shovels coal in a low coal seam. Above, a dock worker loads cotton bales. Trains take goods to market. Electric service extends across much of the state. A business man unfurls plans for future growth. In 1929, Birmingham was the world's largest producer of iron and the South's largest industrial workplace.

O furnace & stoves O furnace workers O coal miner

O dock worker O steam locomotive O electric towers

Birmingham Public Library

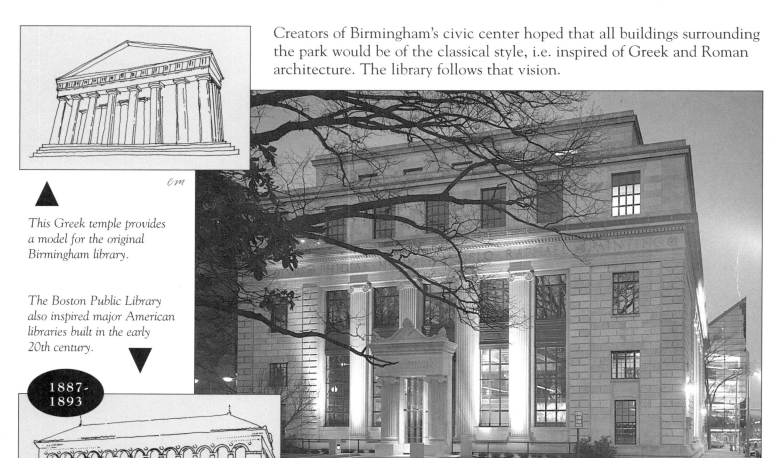

Creators of Birmingham's civic center hoped that all buildings surrounding the park would be of the classical style, i.e. inspired of Greek and Roman architecture. The library follows that vision.

This Greek temple provides a model for the original Birmingham library.

The Boston Public Library also inspired major American libraries built in the early 20th century.

1887-1893

The first Birmingham Public Library, now Linn-Henley Library

The new library

The ancient Greeks and Romans used similar details to ornament their public buildings. A sculptor carved them from blocks of stone.

Find these classical details.

O   scroll bracket

O   acroterion

O   Ionic capital

An inscription (on the Park Place side of the library) states the library's role. What is it?

The Reading Room

The main reading room houses materials relating to Southern history and literature. It's where you go to find your ancestors and study your family roots. You can also find these scenes from world literature.

Name the nationality.

At the fountain of inspiration are Pegasus, a great winged horse, and the poet who captured him with a magic bridle. Pegusus later flew to heaven and became a constellation. _____

A poet and philosopher plucks a petal from a rose tree. He likens his writings to petals saved for his friends from the gardens of his meditations. _____

This ancient wise man appears seated on a dragon. He traveled among the people teaching his ideas of loyalty, righteousness, and humility.

_____

Isis, Goddess of Love and Justice, presents a figure of Truth to her godson Rameses II, who later became a great ruler. His courage in battle inspired one of the first epic poems. _____

Nationalities possible: Chinese, Egyptian, Persian, Roman

New York artist Ezra Winter painted these scenes years ago. They look brilliant and fresh because they were recently cleaned. Conservators dipped cotton swabs in petroleum distillate and removed years of accumulated dirt, then covered the murals with a clear varnish. ▼

Find these heroes.

Murals in the Entrance Hall depict fairy tale hero and heroines.
○ Goldilocks and the Three Bears ○ Jack and the Beanstalk ○ Cinderella

Linn Park

Charles Linn, early banker and manufacturer for whom the park was renamed in the 1980s.

The earliest city plan (1871) included a central park at the head of the main street, 20th Street. In the years since then, the nature of this space had changed dramatically, as the surrounding city grew and changed.

People once lived near the park. Children played here daily. Today the formal space enhances large, orderly public buildings and provides a site for city-wide recreation as well as festivals.

Starting Points:

Birmingham Museum of Art, 2008 Eighth Ave. North. Telephone for tours & school services: 254-2318.

Birmingham Public Library, 2100 Park Place. Telephone for tours K-5th grade: Youth Dept., 226-3655; 6th grade through adults: 226-3604.

Birmingham City Hall, 710 20th St. North. Telephone for hours & tours, Mayor's Office: 254-2283; city council meetings open to the public, Tuesdays, 9:30 a.m.

Jefferson County Courthouse, 716 21st St. North (Richard Arrington, Jr. Blvd. N.). Open weekdays; county commission meetings open to the public, Tuesdays except the 2nd Tuesday every other month, 10:00 a.m.

Hike Area: The park and surrounding civic buildings: city hall, county courthouse, library, museum of art, auditorium and school board offices. Great sites for picnics.

Needed to begin: pencils, quarters for parking meters or fees, tour arrangements at individual sites, curiosity, and at least one hour, not including interior tours.

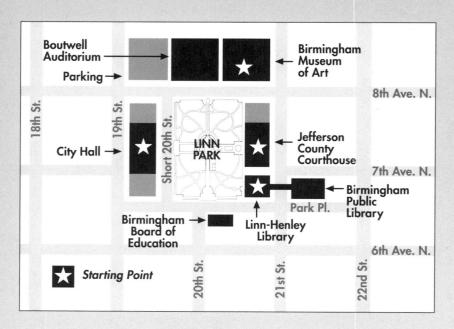

Vocabulary:

Park: from the medieval English and French words meaning enclosure; as in a piece of land in or near a city kept for ornament or recreation.

Recreation: refreshment of strength or health after work; to recreate is to create anew, refresh, restore.

Civic: of or relating to a citizen or to civic affairs.

On the cover: Aerial View of Linn Park, 1993, Jet Lowe, Historic American Engineering Record–National Park Service.

Birmingham Historical Society

Going Downtown

HISTORY HUNT

The Historic Retail & Theater District

Going Downtown

1930s

Third Avenue North at 19th Street

Downtown was the place where people shopped and were entertained. Streetcars, and later automobiles and buses, linked this central theater and retail district to the places people lived. Loveman's, Parisian, Pizitz, Blachs, Burger Phillips, Porters, Saks, and New Ideal — Birmingham's big city stores— thrived on or near 19th Street.

The excitement of shopping store to store kept people coming. The goods and services they wanted were here (and nowhere else). Get someone older than you to describe a day of shopping downtown. Ask these questions:

?

How did you get here?
__ Streetcar   __ Train
__ Bus   __ Auto
__ Train
__ Auto

How did you dress?
__ Dressed up
__ Hats and gloves
__ Heels for ladies

What did you do?
__ Shop for a season
__ Have lunch
__ Go to a sale
__ Go to a parade
__ Go to the movies
__ Window shop

Why did you go?
— Need something
__ To be entertained
__ To hang out

With whom did you go?
__ Your mother   __ Your parents
__ Your grandmother

How long did the visit last?
__ All day   __ All evening
__ All Saturday morning

Was there any other place to shop in Birmingham? _____

What about mail-order catalogs?
__ Sears & Roebuck
__ Montgomery Ward

What happens on 19th Street today?
__ Shopping   __ Movies
— Offices   __ Education

Corner Building

Frank Nelson
Building

KRESS' STORE 5-10-25¢

JACOBS

ORTH CO. ¢10¢

20th St.

1920s

Second Avenue between 19th and 20th Streets

5 and 10 Cent Shopping

S. H. Kress opened the first five-and-ten stores in New York. They quickly spread across America forming the first national chains. Kress sold cheap, standard items in huge volumes for five to ten cents!

 FIND   *Find and circle Kress and Woolworth, another five and ten, in the photograph of Second Avenue above.* ▲

Trade in Birmingham was good. Kress built bigger and bigger stores. The second Kress store on 19th Street also remains today.

 ?

At which national chain stores do you shop? _____

Name stores selling cheap, standard goods. _____

What can you buy for five or ten cents? _____

Parisian Established 1887

Here Birmingham stores looked like their trendy New York and Chicago "cousins:" Saks, Macy's, and Marshall Field.

"We are here with Christmas cheer," reads a Loveman's holiday advertisement. The store's displays brought everyone downtown . . . for window shopping, and sales.

Department Store

Pizitz
Established
1899

Loveman's
Established
1887

1941

These large stores offered many kinds of goods — organized into *departments* — located on multiple floors, all under a single roof.

At one time, Pizitz had 74 departments and 600 employees. They sold almost everything and delivered it to your door.

Sales attracted shoppers. Here they check out fabrics at Loveman's (today's McWane Center).

Name department stores operating in Birmingham today.

_____ _____ _____ _____

Birmingham's Broadway

1900-1960

The performing arts and the movies also found their audiences downtown. More than 70 theaters and movie palaces hosted vaudeville shows, plays, musicals, and movies.

Chaser lights

Loveman's
McWane Center

Marquee

Third Avenue North looking east from 18th Street

Marquees and signs announce store and theater names and purposes. To make sure nobody misses the message, chaser lights trim the elaborate signs.

Movie Mania

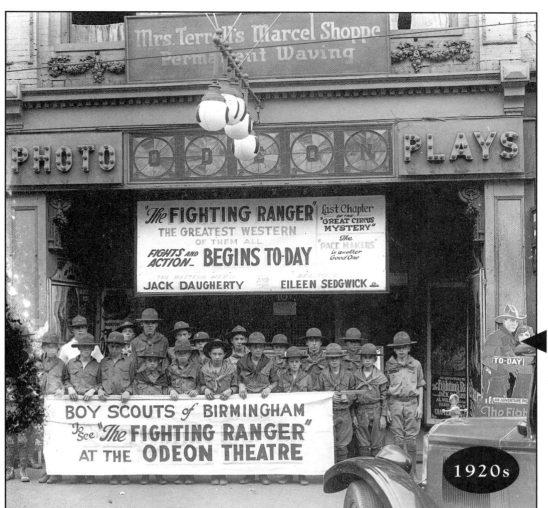

1920s

Competition from radio became fierce, as did the lure of staying home to listen to it. Films and promotions became much more elaborate.

Saturday specials brought school children and scout groups downtown. Movies about the Old West were the rage. ◀

Promotion with the streetcar railways — all of which converged in the downtown area — was a winning strategy to fill the theater seats.

This early Hollywood blockbuster told the story of building the railroads across America. ▶

1924

Palace of the Common Man

Birmingham's and Alabama's largest theater — The Alabama, Showplace of the South — provides splendor for the price of a movie ticket. OPEN TO THE PUBLIC.

Spain, Morocco, and the Orient inspired this fabulous ornament.

This exotic place welcomes 2,500 persons into its world of illusion and fantasy. The Hungarian immigrant who built it wanted his theaters to look like European palaces.

Theater decoration includes African, Asian, and European designs, 9,000 light bulbs, 500 tons of molded plaster and paintings, statuary, and antique furnishings from Spanish castles! The Moorish-style Hall of Mirrors, Oriental Tea Room and English Manor Hall remain rendezvous sites to "Meet Me at The Alabama."

Courtesy The Alabama Theater

Built to show silent movies, The Alabama seats 3,000 persons.

The theater's mighty Wurlitzer organ — with the sound capability of a church organ, a jazz ensemble and a symphony orchestra — fills the palatial interior with marvelous sound.

? **How you seen a movie or attended a concert or a party here lately?**

1927

1926

The Singing Fool, *an early "talkie" that played at The Alabama, featured Al Jolson.*

Movies were silent when The Alabama opened in 1926. A stage orchestra and organ provided the sound effects. Movies and big stage shows from New York changed weekly. Shows and movies, and community functions, continue today, but without costumed ushers.

Decked out in buckskin skirts and feathers, these ushers welcome moviegoers to the Lyric Theater.

Fancy Detail
Scavenger Hunt

During the early 20th century, store and shop owners considered their buildings a gift to the street. Skilled craftsmen created highly decorated building fronts. Look up to find these details.

**Hunt Location: 200 Block 19th Street
1800 Block Third Avenue North**

Find these details.

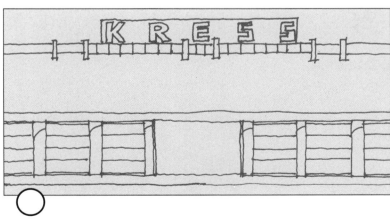

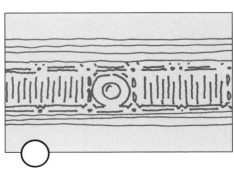

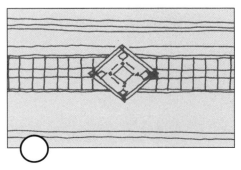

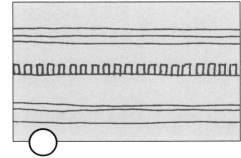

Going Downtown

The parade route went right up 19th Street, with merchants and everyone pitching in to celebrate civic causes.

In the early 20th century, 19th Street became the center of downtown shopping and entertainment. Independent merchants and later immense department stores and national chains offered clothes and shoes, and everything needed for the home.

Comedies, operas, melodramas, minstrel shows, serious theater and the movies played in the lavish theaters and "picture" palaces, known as *Birmingham's Broadway*.

Starting Points:

McWane Center, formerly Loveman's Department Store, 200-16th St. North. Telephone for tours: 714-8414.
Alabama Theater, 1811 Third Ave. North. Telephone for tours: 251- 0418.

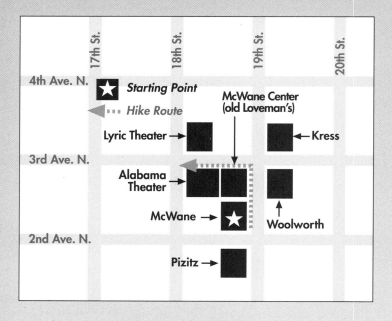

Hike Area: 200 Block 19th Street & 1800 Block Third Ave. North

Needed to begin: pencils, quarters for parking meters or fees, tour arrangements at individual sites, curiosity and a half an hour, not including site tours.

Vocabulary:

Broadway: a street in New York City near many of that city's legitimate theaters and playhouses
Department store: a store selling a wide variety of goods arranged in many departments
Vaudeville: stage entertainment consisting of unrelated acts such as music, dancing, acrobats, pantomime and comics.

BIRMINGHAM HISTORICAL SOCIETY

Fourth Avenue

HISTORY HUNT

THE HISTORIC BLACK BUSINESS DISTRICT

Northside

Homes and churches crowd the area just west of the main business district along the 20th Street spine. Here blacks lived, worshipped, and did business. Many others from across the city gathered here for social and business events.

Sixth Avenue leads past homes and churches to Kelly Ingram Park and 20th Street.
The emerging Fourth Avenue district is to the top right. It's wash day. Clotheslines are fully hung.

1930s

1950s

The Knights of Pythias posed for this photograph at the Lyric Theater, across the street from their headquarters.

Sorority women meet at Sixteenth Street Baptist Church to discuss community service projects. Ruth L. Jackson presides.

The Business District

Fourth Avenue emerged as *the* commercial and social center for black patrons in the 1910s. Jim Crow laws required the separation of the races and located black businesses here.

Banks, barber and beauty shops, restaurants, theaters, hotels, funeral homes, and photographic studios thrived until desegregation in the 1960s. In the 1990s black business began a comeback.

*"That's where he came up,
where he strived,
where he got financed
and could appreciate life."*

1930s

Fourth Avenue, looking west from 19th Street.

1913

The Penny Savings Bank, one of four black-owned banks in the city, encouraged savings and provided money for buying homes and businesses.

1937

1939

Tom's Real Shine, though tiny, was well located at a bus stop, where people waited. Tom is dressed in white.

Elsie Bradford operated the Bradford Funeral Home here from 1908 until 1941. Her hearse is a Cadillac equipped with a full-length flower tray.

Let Me Entertain You

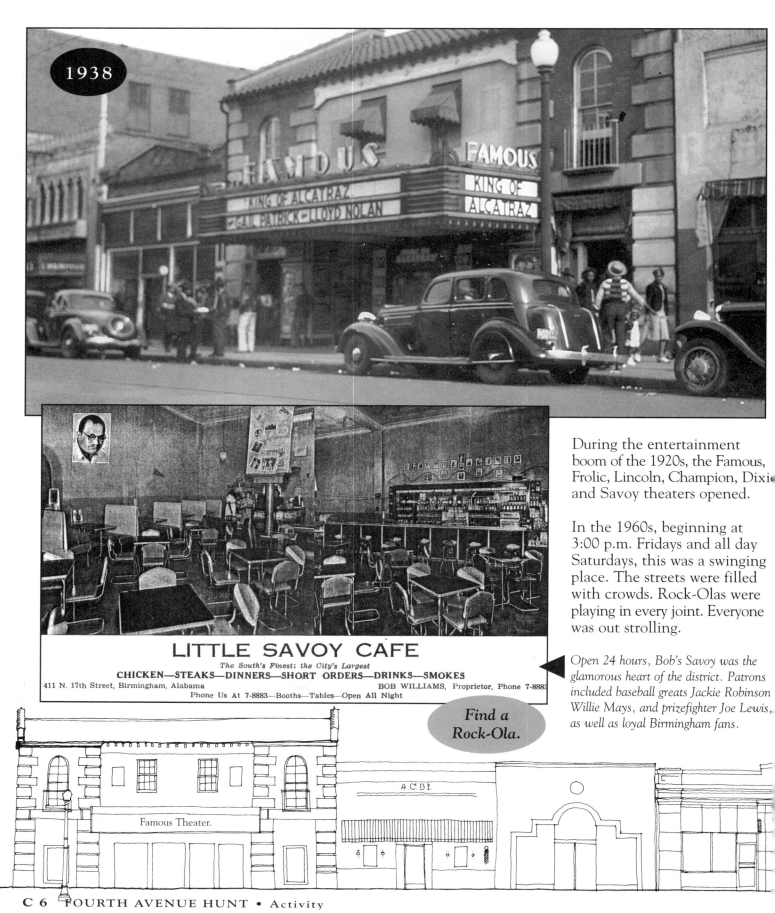

1938

FAMOUS
KING OF ALCATRAZ
GAIL PATRICK and LLOYD NOLAN

FAMOUS
KING OF ALCATRAZ

LITTLE SAVOY CAFE
The South's Finest; the City's Largest
CHICKEN—STEAKS—DINNERS—SHORT ORDERS—DRINKS—SMOKES
411 N. 17th Street, Birmingham, Alabama   BOB WILLIAMS, Proprietor, Phone 7-8883
Phone Us At 7-8883—Booths—Tables—Open All Night

During the entertainment boom of the 1920s, the Famous, Frolic, Lincoln, Champion, Dixie and Savoy theaters opened.

In the 1960s, beginning at 3:00 p.m. Fridays and all day Saturdays, this was a swinging place. The streets were filled with crowds. Rock-Olas were playing in every joint. Everyone was out strolling.

Open 24 hours, Bob's Savoy was the glamorous heart of the district. Patrons included baseball greats Jackie Robinson Willie Mays, and prizefighter Joe Lewis, as well as loyal Birmingham fans.

Find a Rock-Ola.

Famous Theater.

A.C.B.E.

Business As Usual

Built to show movies, the Carver Theater is now the place to learn about jazz. The Alabama Jazz Hall of Fame presents exhibits and live performances.
OPEN TO THE PUBLIC.

Find these signs and details.

Fourth Avenue's one- and two-story buildings provide a lively place for doing business and for gathering.

Possible types of businesses on Fourth Avenue & in the 300 blocks of 17th & 18th Streets:

Count the businesses.

___ banks ___ barbers ___ food ___ offices ___ entertainment ___ insurance
___ lawyers ___ other _____

Visitor Center—Urban Impact

The Masonic Temple

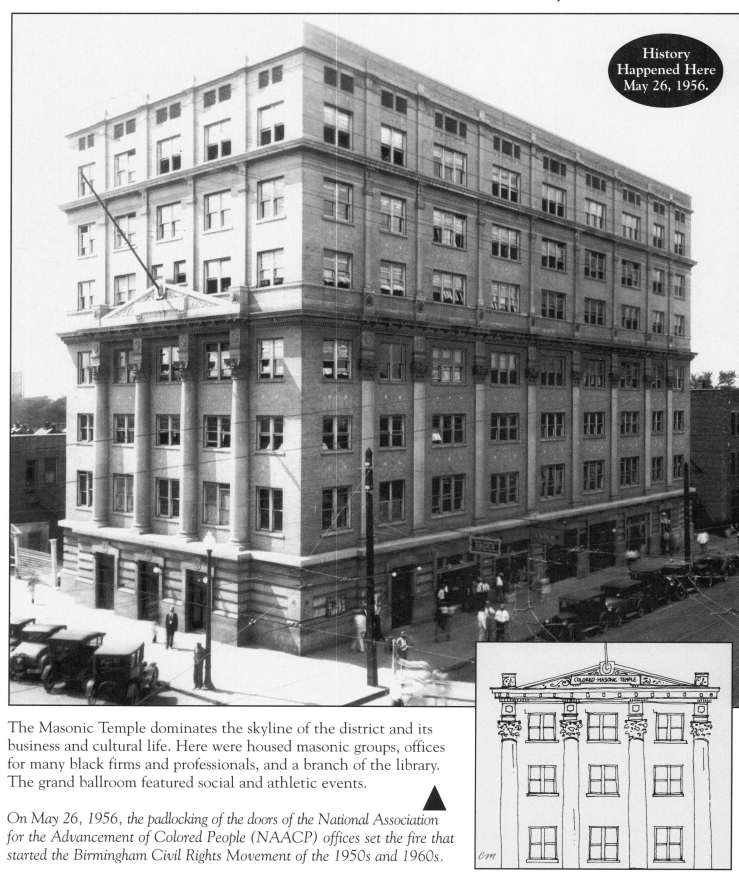

History Happened Here May 26, 1956.

The Masonic Temple dominates the skyline of the district and its business and cultural life. Here were housed masonic groups, offices for many black firms and professionals, and a branch of the library. The grand ballroom featured social and athletic events.

On May 26, 1956, the padlocking of the doors of the National Association for the Advancement of Colored People (NAACP) offices set the fire that started the Birmingham Civil Rights Movement of the 1950s and 1960s.

1930s

Jazz Alive

In the Masonic Temple's dance hall, big bands and big name performers played to packed houses.

Duke Ellington and his band performed here regularly.

Count Basie's recordings and endless travel reinforced his international fame. He played the Masonic Temple annually.

? Which musicians play Birmingham today?

_____

Where do they play?

_____

1930s 1940s

The chimes of a vibraphone contributed to the mellow sound of Birmingham musician Fess Whatley and his Vibra Cathedral Band.

John T. ("Fess") Whatley, band instructor at Parker High School, was a nationally known musician and teacher. His students played with America's best big bands.

Big Bands

Birmingham native Erskine Hawkins performs in a playful style with his Alabama State Collegians as they record, live and on stage, for a radio audience.

Hawkins' song about an Ensley dance hall (as arranged by Glenn Miller) became an international hit.

Come on down, forget your care.
Come on down, I'll see you there.
Tuxedo Junction, now.

1939

Singing his dreamy 1964 hit "The Way You Do The Things You Do" is Birmingham's Eddie Kendricks. A classy dresser, the tall, handsome tenor sang leads for The Temptations, a male vocal group with 37 Top Ten hits in the 1960s. The Birmingham News.

Fourth Avenue

Prior to 1900, a black business district did not exist. In a pattern characteristic of Southern cities founded after the Civil War, blacks developed businesses alongside those of whites in many sections of the city center.

In the early 20th century, Jim Crow laws authorizing the distinct separation of the races and subsequent restrictions forced the growing black businesses into the area in and about Fourth Avenue. Here banks and insurance firms, restaurants, theaters and hotels, barbers and beauty shops, and funeral homes flourished. Jazz, big bands, vaudeville shows, and the movies played to packed houses. Fourth Avenue had it all.

Starting Points:

Alabama Jazz Hall of Fame-Carver Performing Arts Theater, 1631 Fourth Ave. North. Telephone for tours: 254-2731 or 254-2720.

Historical Fourth Avenue Visitor Information Center-Urban Impact, Inc., Fourth & 17th. Telephone for district tours: 328-1850.

Masonic Temple, 1630 Fourth Ave. North. Telephone for permission to visit the ballroom (Access is provided by the elevator operator.) Call the Grand Master's office: 328-9078.

Or continue from the *Going Downtown Hunt* or *A Walk to Freedom*.

Hike Area: 1700 Block Fourth Ave. North, 300 Blocks of 17th & 18th Streets

Needed to begin: pencils, quarters for parking meters or fees, tour arrangements at individual sites, curiosity and at least an hour.

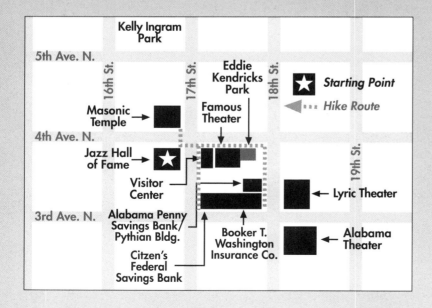

Vocabulary:

Racial zoning-the arranging or dividing into zones by race; division sanctioned by laws

Rock-Ola or jukebox-a coin-operated boom box of the 1950s & 1960s (with built-in tunes)

Segregation-separation or isolation of a race, enforced by laws and other barriers to social interaction

The Temptations-a popular Motown (motor-town=Detroit) singing group of the 1960s

On the cover:
The King Oliver Band, *Vaudeville, California, 1922.*

Dr A. G. Gaston, (1893-1996) There was nothing Dr. Gaston could not sell. He built a business empire: burial policies, insurance, banking and construction firms, funeral homes and cemeteries, a motel, restaurant, and business college. Booker T. Washington Insurance Co.

BIRMINGHAM HISTORICAL SOCIETY

A Walk to Freedom

HISTORY HUNT

STUDENT BATTLES FOR CIVIL RIGHTS, MAY & SEPTEMBER 1963

We started this battle and we mean to go through ...

During April and May of 1963, thousands of men, women, and children demonstrated for freedom. They faced water hoses and police dogs, without violence in return. Their story is a remarkable story of people of stalwart faith who believed that God would help them in their all-out, nonviolent confrontation to banish segregation. They walked together, endured and suffered, until Freedom was won for all Americans through the passage of the Civil Rights Act of 1964. (This act guaranteed participation in public accommodations: schools, stores, restaurants, theaters, and transportation facilities.)

For seven years prior to the events in the spring of 1963, despite numerous bombings and constant threats and intimidation from the Klu Klux Klan and the police, the Rev. Fred Shuttlesworth and the Alabama Christian Movement for Human Rights (ACMHR) created the strongest Southern civil rights organization and challenged every segregation law. ACMHR was led by Shuttlesworth's Bethel Baptist Church and 59 other black churches, whose membership of preachers, deacons, Sunday school teachers, secretaries, blue collar workers and their children supported the organization with pennies or, at most, a dollar or two a week.

Students from Miles and Daniel Payne Colleges assisted as early as 1960 when they organized the first (and one of several very successful) boycotts of downtown stores. Students led the Freedom Rides of 1961 and later sit-ins in Birmingham and across the South. And in the spring of 1963, they helped organize and participate in the marches. Initially, high school and college students were to demonstrate, but many arrived with their little brothers and sisters who insisted on their right to join the fight for freedom. For seven days, the children marched until the jails, and the television newscasts, were filled. Their protests set in gear the Civil Rights Act of 1964.

Few times in our history has a group of ordinary men, women, and children risked life and limb so unremittingly for the purpose of achieving liberty and equality. Birmingham can be proud its citizens won the battle for freedom on its streets.

Retrace their steps. It's May 6, 1963, the night before the final march. Join the battle against segregation. Demonstrate for freedom.

I'm on my way to freedom land.

I'm on my way . . . *I'm on my way . . .*
    to freedom land . . . *to freedom land.*
I'm on my way, Oh Lord, to freedom land.
    Chorus, repeat twice.

If you don't go, don't hinder me.
It's an up-hill journey.
There is nothing you can do, to turn me around.
I asked my mother, come and go with me.
If my mother don't go, I go anyhow.
Are you on your way, to Freedom Land? *Chorus*

Yes, we want out freedom.

Yes, we want our freedom.
Yes, we want to volunteer.
Yes, we want our freedom.
We want our freedom and we want it now.
    Chorus, repeat thrice.

I'm traveling down in Birmingham,
    praying to the Lord all the time.
But we have made up our mind to travel on,
    because freedom can't turn us down. *Chorus.*

The cops can't stop us. The mob can't stop us.
    In the middle of the night and the daytime too,
    we started this battle and we mean to go through.
    Chorus, repeat twice.

Folklorists recorded Birmingham's Movement Choir singing these freedom songs at an ACMHR Mass Meeting on May 6, 1963. Everyone in the 1960s knew them. Singing them brought courage, unity and the resolve.

Yes, we want our freedom, I'm on my way to freedom land. Traditional, words and music arranged by Carlton Reese, Director, ACMHR Movement Choir. Reprinted with Permission of Carlton Reese from *SING FOR FREEDOM-The Story of the Civil Rights Movement through its songs,* a 1990 Smithsonian/Folkways Recording.

Take the pledge.

The Non-Violence Ethic

ACMHR Pledge

I HEREBY PLEDGE MYSELF, MY PERSON AND BODY, TO THE NONVIOLENT MOVEMENT. THEREFORE, I WILL KEEP THE FOLLOWING TEN COMMANDMENTS:

1. MEDITATE daily on the teachings and life of Jesus.
2. REMEMBER always that the nonviolent movement in Birmingham seeks justice and reconciliation – not victory.
3. WALK and TALK in the manner of love, for God is love.
4. PRAY daily to be used by God in order that all men might be free.
5. SACRIFICE personal wishes in order that all men might be free.
6. OBSERVE with both friend and foe the ordinary rules of courtesy.
7. SEEK to perform regular service for others and for the world.
8. REFRAIN from the violence of fist, tongue, or heart.
9. STRIVE to be in good spiritual and bodily health.
10. FOLLOW the directions of the movement and the captain on a demonstration.

I sign this pledge, having seriously considered what I do and with the determination and will to persevere.

Name _____

Besides demonstrations, I could also help the Movement by: (Circle the proper items) Run errands, Drive my car, Fix food for volunteers, Clerical work, Make phone calls, Answer phones, Mimeograph, Type, Print signs, Distribute leaflets.

Alabama Christian Movement for Human Rights
Birmingham Affiliate of S. C. L. C. • F. L. Shuttlesworth, President

Southern Christian Leadership Conference (SCLC) officers, the Reverends Fred Shuttlesworth, Ralph Abernathy, and Martin Luther King, Jr., left to right, in work shirts highlighting the boycott of white stores, led the march on Good Friday, April 12, 1963. Reverend King and SCLC had come to Birmingham to assist Shuttlesworth's ACMHR with their segregation protests. Birmingham Police Department Surveillance Files, Birmingham Public Library Department of Archives and Manuscripts 1125.11.20 A-1.

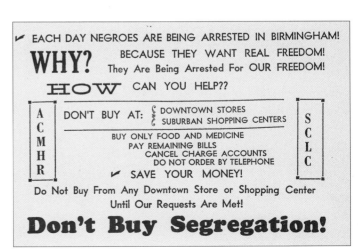

✔ EACH DAY NEGROES ARE BEING ARRESTED IN BIRMINGHAM!

WHY? BECAUSE THEY WANT REAL FREEDOM! They Are Being Arrested For OUR FREEDOM!

HOW CAN YOU HELP??

A C M H R

DON'T BUY AT: { DOWNTOWN STORES { SUBURBAN SHOPPING CENTERS

BUY ONLY FOOD AND MEDICINE
PAY REMAINING BILLS
CANCEL CHARGE ACCOUNTS
DO NOT ORDER BY TELEPHONE

✔ SAVE YOUR MONEY!

S C L C

Do Not Buy From Any Downtown Store or Shopping Center Until Our Requests Are Met!

Don't Buy Segregation!

Courtesy Lola Hendricks

Keep This Movement Moving

Thank you very kindly, my very dear friends. These churches are really loaded tonight. Never in the history of this nation, have so many people been arrested for the cause of freedom and human dignity. You know there are approximately 25 hundred people in jail, right now.

Now, let me say this. The thing that we are challenged to do, is to keep this Movement moving. There is power in unity and there is power in numbers. As long as we keep moving like we are moving, the power structure of Birmingham will have to give in. And we are probably nearer to a solution of this problem than we are able to realize.

And don't worry about your children, they are going to be all right. Don't hold them back if they want to go to jail. For they are doing a job for not only for themselves, but for all America and for all mankind.

Somewhere we read. "A little child shall lead them." Remember, there was another little child, just 12 years old, and he got involved in a discussion back in Jerusalem, as his parents moved down the dusty road leading them back to their little village in Nazareth. And when they got back and bothered him and touched him and wanted him to move on, he said, 'I must be about my Father's business.'

These young people are about their Father's business, and they are carving a tunnel of hope through the Red Mountain of despair and they will bring to this nation a newness and a genuine quality and an idealism that it so desperately needs.

Now, we are going to see that they are treated right. Don't worry about that. The Justice Department is already in here. And they don't have some small fish from the Justice Department. They have some of the big fish in here.

And we are reminding them, at all times, that these persons are political prisoners. And there is a distinction between a political prisoner and somebody who's in for being out to get drunk and somebody there engaging in a robbery. And we are going to see that they are treated right. We're going to fill up the jails around here and we're going to fill up the jails all over Alabama, if necessary. . . .

Keep this Movement going. Keep coming. If you can't fly, run. If you can't run, walk. If you can't walk, crawl. But by all means, keep moving.

The Rev. Martin Luther King, Jr. speaking at an Alabama Christian Movement for Human Rights, May 6, 1963. As recorded on the Sing for Freedom CD. License granted by Intellectual Properties Management, Inc., Atlanta, Georgia, as manager of the King Estate.

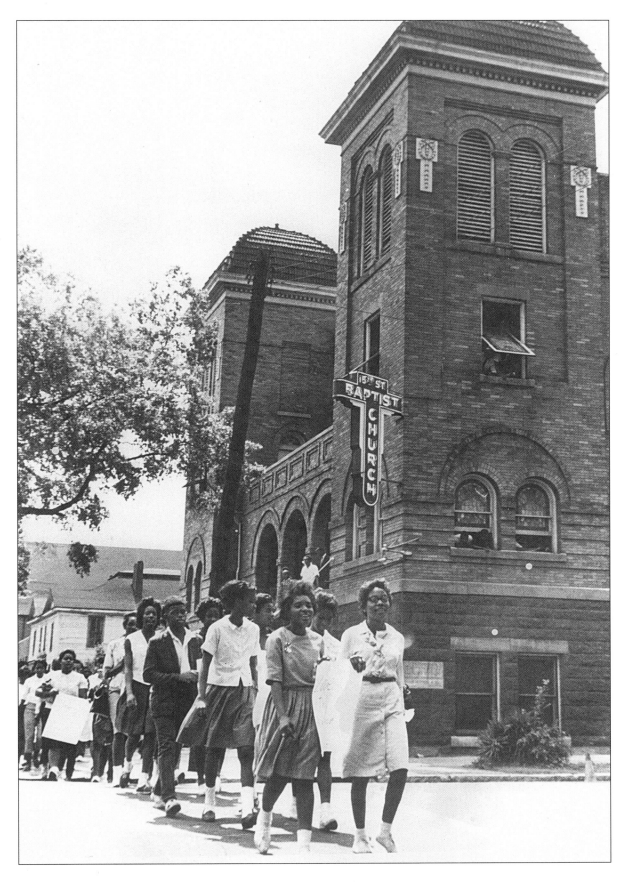

The children's marches began May 2, 1963 with 1,000 students leaving school to protest segregation. Following training in nonviolence at St. Paul's Methodist, St. John AME and Sixteenth Street Baptist Church, in groups of 30 to 60, they emerged singing freedom songs. Most were arrested as they moved east along Sixth Avenue. Ten groups made it to City Hall to pray for their civil rights. UPI/Corbis Bettman U1378400-6, reprinted with permission.

They turned on the water hoses ...

On May 3 and 4, orderly groups of students streamed again from downtown churches. Birmingham Commissioner of Public Safety Bull Connor ordered firemen to use stronger water to stop the demonstrators. The firemen's high pressure hoses could knock marchers off their feet from as far away as 50 yards. Hoses were equipped with monitor guns—devices that permitted two hoses to form one spray. UPI/Corbis Bettman Archive UI378208-29, reprinted with permission.

Hoses to face.
Kelly Ingram Park

Dogs to face.

Kelly Ingram Park

Birmingham police used dogs to control crowds and disperse demonstrators as the television cameras rolled. President John Kennedy stated that the sight of the assaults in Birmingham made him sick, and that now he could "well understand why the Negroes of Birmingham are tired of being asked to be patient." National TV viewers echoed the President's revulsion to police and firemen using dogs and hoses on children. Birmingham Public Library Archives 1076.1.26.

> Now, You know what happened Easter Sunday, they brought the dogs out, turned them a loose on our people. You know what happened last Friday, they brought the dogs out, and they tore the garments from our people. They turned the water hoses on. But what happened yesterday to the dogs? They still have those same dogs. They still have the water hoses and the water, but they didn't use it.
>
> We have already won a victory here in Birmingham. And all we got to do is to keep marching. Do tomorrow what we did today, and do it the next day. And then the next day we won't have to do it at all, because yesterday, we filled–day before yesterday–up the jails. And then today, we filled up the jail yard. And on tomorrow, when they look up and see that number coming, I don't know what they're going do.

Ralph Abernathy speaking at a Mass Meeting, May 6, 1963, as recorded on *Sing for Freedom*, reprinted with permission of Mrs. Ralph Abernathy.

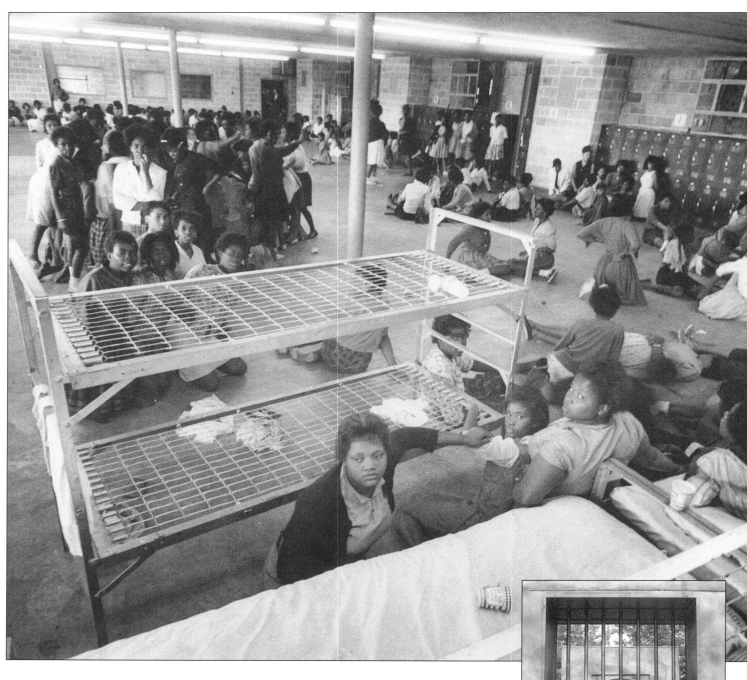

With more than 2,500 persons jailed for freedom, city and county jails in Birmingham and Bessemer, the 4-H Barracks at the fairgrounds, and many other temporary shelters were full. In this photograph, students wait for transport to makeshift jails in a Basement Room at Birmingham City Hall. The jail is recreated in a Kelly Ingram Park sculpture.Charles Moore, Black Star. Reprinted with permission.

How does jail feel?

By May 6, march organizers had the drill down pat. In the morning, more than 2,000 students arrived to march for freedom. Just after noon, they marched long enough to fill the footage for the nightly television newscasts, often proceeding a single block to school buses waiting at 17th Street to pick them up. In marching that one block, they filled sufficient footage to accomplish a media coup. The students had won the war: Americans would no longer tolerate segregation. In the photograph above, police arrest the students near the Alabama Theater. Birmingham Public Library Archives, The Birmingham News Collection 1076.1.32.

Schools Desegregate

During the summer of 1963, President John Kennedy introduced the bill that would become the national civil rights act. Rev. Martin Luther King, Jr., led the March on Washington to generate national support for desegregation laws and Birmingham officials labored to comply with court decisions to desegregate schools and other public facilities. Meanwhile, Alabama Governor George Wallace, other public officials, and rabble-rousers encouraged protests and disregard for the law.

On September 4, 1963, honor roll students Dwight and Floyd Armstrong, ages 11 and 10, registered at the all-white Graymont School in the Smithfield neighborhood. The Reverend Shuttlesworth, far right; their father, James Armstrong, center, and attorneys accompanied them. (Today, the boys, their wives and their children are college graduates, doctors, and lawyers.) The Birmingham News, September 5, 1963.

Children Sacrifice

The dynamite blast at Sixteenth Street Baptist Church on Sunday, September 15, 1963 at 10:22 a.m. sounded an alarm heard round the world. Now everyone could understand the atrocity and the hate that prevented desegregation.

Four little girls — Addie Mae Collins, 14; Denise McNair, 11; Cynthia Diane Wesley, 14; and Carole Rosamond Robertson, 14 — sacrificed their lives for freedom. Their sacrifice hastened the passage of the National Civil Rights Act of 1964.

Officer with Bayonet Helps Maintain Order, 16th Street Baptist Church, September 15, 1963, The Birmingham News.

A Walk to Freedom

It's May 6, 1963, thousands of students are skipping school to join the freedom marches, face water hoses and police dogs, and go to jail. Join the fight for freedom. Fill the jail yard. Help pass the Civil Rights Act of 1964 and learn of the sacrifices Birmingham children made to win our freedom.

This booklet, together with a Smithsonian/Folkways recording made the night before the final freedom march of 1963, provides historic photographs, songs and speeches to retrace the marchers' footsteps. Learn nonviolent procedure, sing freedom songs, and listen to inspirational talks by the Reverends Martin Luther King, Jr,. and Ralph Abernathy, and then face the dogs and hoses, now recreated as sculpture in Kelly Ingram Park.

Starting Points:

Birmingham Civil Rights Institute, 520 16th St. North. Telephone for tours & special programs: 328-9696.

Sixteenth Street Baptist Church, 1530 Sixth Ave. North., across Sixth Avenue from the Institute. The church and the Institute face Kelly Ingram Park. Telephone for tours: 251-9402.

Hike Area: 16th Street to Kelly Ingram Park, located between 5th & 6th Aves. North, 16th & 17th Streets.

Needed to begin: A CD player and *SING FOR FREEDOM-The stories of the Civil Rights Movement through its songs*, a Smithsonian/Folkways Recording, 1990, compiled with notes by Guy and Candie Carawab, available from SI. edu.folkways, 202-275-1144. The Birmingham recording of King and Abernathy's speeches and the ACMHR Movement Choir directed by Carlton Reese was made May 6, 1963.

Useful: *A Walk to Freedom-The Reverend Fred Shuttlesworth and the Alabama Christian Movement for Human Rights, 1956-1964* available from Birmingham Historical Society. (This is a pictorial chronology.)

Vocabulary:

Alabama Christian Movement for Human Rights (ACMHR)-established in 1956 as a local organization with a mission to obtain freedom and first-class citizenship for Birmingham blacks; the strongest local desegregation organization, headed by the Rev. Fred Shuttlesworth from 1956 until 1969.

The Civil Rights Act of 1964-federal law providing for equal treatment in public accommodations: schools, restaurants, stores, transportation facilities, etc.

Freedom-the state of being free, the absence of constraint in choice or conduct.

Martin Luther King, Jr. (1929-1968), charismatic leader of the American Civil Right Movement of the 1960s.

Nonviolence-abstaining from or free of violence.

Fred Shuttlesworth (1922-)-energetic Freedom Fighter, longtime president of ACMHR, the organization that broke the back of segregation in Birmingham and the nation; longtime secretary and member of the inner circle of SCLC.

Southern Christian Leadership Conference (SCLC)-established in 1957, Reverend King's network of organizations, the union of local segregation groups, such as ACMHR.

On the cover: Singing school children head out from Sixteenth Street Baptist Church, just after noon. Some march across Kelly Ingram Park to the retail district, others to City Hall, May 3, 1963. UPI/Corbis-Bettmann 1378209.29. Reprinted with permission.

Map labels:
St. John A.M.E. Church — 15th St. — 16th St. — 17th St. — 7th Ave. N.
St. Paul (United) Methodist Church — 16th St. Bapt. Church
To City Hall — 6th Ave. N.
Birmingham Civil Rights Institute
A.G. Gaston Motel
KELLY INGRAM PARK
5th Ave. N.
To Retail District
★ Starting Point
◄ Hike Route